The Book of Kali

IN THE SAME SERIES

The Book of Devi by Bulbul Sharma

The Book of Vishnu by Nanditha Krishna

The Book of Shiva by Namita Gokhale

The Book of Krishna by Pavan K. Varma

The Book of Ganesha by Royina Grewal

The Book of Durga by Nilima Chitgopekar

The Book of Muhammad by Mehru Jaffer

The Book of Nanak by Navtej Sarna

ALSO AVAILABLE FROM PENGUIN

The Names of Allah by Parvez Dewan

Hymns of the Gurus translated by Khushwant Singh

The Hanuman Chalisa of Goswami Tulasi Das translated by Parvez Dewan

Rehras: Evensong—The Sikh Evening Prayer translated by Reema Anand and Khushwant Singh

The Name of My Beloved: Verses of the Sikh Gurus translated by Nikky Guninder Kaur Singh

The Book of Prayer compiled and edited by Renuka Narayanan

The Book of
Kali

SEEMA MOHANTY

PENGUIN
ANANDA

An imprint of Penguin Random House

PENGUIN ANANDA

USA | Canada | UK | Ireland | Australia
New Zealand | India | South Africa | China | Singapore

Penguin Ananda is part of the Penguin Random House group of companies
whose addresses can be found at global.penguinrandomhouse.com

Published by Penguin Random House India Pvt. Ltd
4th Floor, Capital Tower 1, MG Road,
Gurugram 122 002, Haryana, India

First published in Viking by Penguin Books India 2004

Published in Penguin Books 2009

Text copyright © Seema Mohanty 2004

Illustrations copyright © Devdutt Pattanaik 2004

Illustrations by Devdutt Pattanaik

All rights reserved

10 9 8 7 6 5 4 3 2

ISBN 9780143419914

Typeset in Sabon by Mantra Virtual Services, New Delhi
Printed at Manipal Technologies Limited, India

www.penguin.co.in

This is a legitimate digitally printed version of the book and therefore might not
have certain extra finishing on the cover.

To my family
who has always been there

Contents

Introduction

Her outstretched tongue distinguishes her from all other goddesses in the Hindu pantheon. Her nakedness, unbound hair, association with blood and gore, and unbridled sexuality challenge conventional ideas of divinity. So much so that, to the uninformed eye Kali appears less as a manifestation of the divine, and more as a bloodthirsty ogress—a patron of thugs and sorcerers.

In the quest to understand Kali, it is essential to appreciate the Hindu concept of the divine. Hindus visualize the divine in various forms—human, animal, plant and mineral. Each form, with its respective narrative and rituals, serves as a gateway to realizing the ultimate unmanifest godhead. Worshippers of Shiva and Vishnu, the two most popular male manifestations of the divine, believe that the male form of the divine represents spiritual reality, while the female form symbolizes material reality. Goddess worshippers, however, associate both material and spiritual realities with the female form. To them, Kali is both Goddess or Devi (the female divinity, the supreme manifestation of the divine) and goddess (one of the several incarnations of Devi). As 'Goddess' Kali embodies both spiritiual and material realities, the totality of nature, as she creates, sustains and destroys the world. As 'goddess' Kali represents only that aspect of material reality, which is wild and untamed, she complements Gauri, the radiant and gentle goddess who represents the domesticated and tamed manifestation of nature.

Worship of the Goddess in India is as ancient as civilization itself, and has its roots in the belief that the earth is a living being that nourishes all animate objects. The most widely accepted theory states that when the nomadic cattle-herding Aryans assimilated with the settled agricultural communities of the Indian subcontinent almost 4000 years ago, the male-dominated, sky-gazing Vedic deities mingled and merged with the local female-dominated, earthbound, Dravidian (some may say pre-Aryan tantrik) divinities. From this fusion rose the goddesses of India who populate not just the Hindu pantheon but also Jain and Buddhist mythologies.

It is difficult to trace the history of Kali worship in India. Even before the name Kali was first documented in scriptures, there are references of goddesses (and demonesses) that allude to Kali. For example, in the *Rig Samhita* there is Nirriti, a dark goddess associated with death, who was feared and needed to be appeased. In the *Jaiminya Brahmana*, there is a verse celebrating the triumph of Indra over Dirgha-jihvi, a long-tongued and lascivious ogress, who thirsts for the divine drink Soma.

It is also difficult to trace the extent of Kali worship in India. In villages across India, goddesses are classified as 'hot' and 'cold'. Hot goddesses are wild and angry, threatening communities with drought and epidemic unless appeased by blood sacrifice. Cold goddesses are gentle and domestic, who nurture communities with love and tenderness. Hot goddesses like Bhagavati of Kerala and Yellamma of Karnataka are sometimes referred to as Kali but do not have the characteristic outstretched tongue. At the same time there are goddesses such as Korravai, the naked Tamil goddess of war, and Chamunda, the emaciated goddess of crematoriums, who share Kali's association with blood sacrifices, death and exorcism but do not share her name.

Narratives, symbols and rituals associated with Kali invariably overlap with those of other goddesses. Also, what applies to Kali in one part of India need not apply elsewhere. Further, what was true about Kali in yesteryears may not be true today. All this makes it difficult to define boundaries in the study of Kali.

Kali is but one of the many goddesses of India, though undoubtedly the most popular. Her fame owes a great deal to European Imperialism of the eighteenth and nineteenth century as well as Radical Feminism of the twentieth century. While for the former, this exotic and 'ghoulish' deity validated the urgent need to convert and civilize the natives, for the latter, this defiant goddess was a manifestation of the female collective unconscious that sought liberation from male-dominated regimes.

Despite her popularity, Kali remains an enigma to

most people, including Hindus. Her macabre persona defies explanation and forces one to be defensive or apologetic. This book makes a conscious effort to unconditionally accept the stories, images and rituals through which the idea of Kali has been communicated over the ages. By doing so, it hopes to decode the meaning behind the macabre, and help the reader gain an insight into the Hindu approach to the divine.

The Form

Hindus project the idea of God in a variety of forms. Each form brings together a set of symbols that communicate the Hindu understanding of life and divinity. Ideally, since God is believed to be an absolute entity and the container of all things, there must be only one form of God that projects every conceivable universal idea simultaneously. But this is impossible to achieve. Hence, Hindus have many gods and goddesses, each evoking one aspect of divinity. The ascetic Shiva, for example, evokes world-renouncing ideas while the regal Vishnu evokes world-affirming ideas. Durga, who dresses as a bride but functions as a killer, communicates the principles of sex and violence that make the cycle of life go round. The form of Kali and its constituent symbols are meant to evoke bhaya and vibhitsa—fear and revulsion—forcing the observer to acknowledge the dark and unpleasant aspects of the cosmos—and hence of the divine—that one often tries to deny, repress or suppress.

Every description of Kali, after giving allowances to regional and temporal variations, has certain commonalities. She is invariably dark, naked and with unbound and dishevelled hair. She stands on Shiva's chest, holds in her hands a bloodstained scythe and a human head, has a garland of male heads around her neck and a girdle of hands around her waist. Her tongue is outstretched and smeared with blood. Surrounded by corpses, dogs and jackals, her stance looks threatening. There is no denying the fact that Kali makes an impact on the observer.

Outstretched tongue

There are many goddesses who like Kali are naked and associated with blood and death. These include Chandi, Chamunda, Bhairavi and Bhagavati. But what distinguishes Kali from other goddesses is her outstretched tongue. In some narratives, Kali spreads her tongue to drink the blood of the demon Rakta-bija before it touches the ground and sprouts Rakta-bija clones. In other narratives, Kali sticks out her tongue in embarrassment on realizing that she has stepped on her own husband in her bloodlust. In Kali temples, the tongue is smeared with the blood of sacrificed animals. With the outstretched tongue, Kali teases and mocks her devotees—she sees through their social façade and knows the dark desires they try so hard to deny or suppress. She provokes them to delve into their subconscious and confront all those memories and thoughts that they shy away from.

In many parts of India, the image of Kali does not have the characteristic outstretched tongue, though she may have fangs protruding from the corners of her mouth. This form is called Bhadra-Kali, or the 'decent Kali' who does not reject feminine grace totally. She resides in household shrines and serves as the guardian of the family.

Dark complexion

The word kali means 'black'. Kali is associated with all things black—her skin is dark, her hair black, her priests wear black, she is worshipped on new moon 'black' nights, and she is often portrayed in the company of black cats. She defies all that a fair complexion stands for—domestication, gentleness and beauty. The Goddess, or Devi, sheds her dark Kali form and becomes Gauri, who is gaur or fair, only when asked to marry Shiva.

Artists often paint Kali not black but purple or blue. Generally, the black Kali is called Smashana-Kali and enshrined in crematoria, while the blue or purple Kali is called Bhadra-Kali or Dakshina-Kali and worshipped in household and community shrines. Purple, blue or black, Kali refuses to endorse traditional concepts of beauty and auspiciousness.

Unbound hair

In traditional Hindu families, the unmarried virgin plaits her hair, the married woman oils, combs, parts and knots her hair, while the widow is made to shave her hair. Hair is thus a metaphor for sexuality—poised for fulfilment in the virgin, domesticated and controlled in the married woman, and stripped away in the widow. Kali's hair is dishevelled and unbound, indicating that her sexuality is unfettered by social norms. She represents the wild, untamed aspects of the forest—a site where sex and violence are unbridled, governed primarily by the quest for survival.

In narratives, Devi always unbinds her hair when angry or upset, or when she is called to battle. In the Tantrik Mahabharata, the untying of Draupadi's hair by the Kauravas marks the collapse of civilized conduct. Things are restored when Draupadi ties her hair after washing it with Kaurava blood after the carnage on the battlefield of Kurukshetra.

Garland of heads, girdle of arms

Kali wears around her neck a garland of human heads. These are invariably those of men, moustached and virile-looking. In one Telegu folk tradition, the heads around Kali's neck belong to a demon who had received the boon that no sooner did any of his heads touch the ground than the world would burst into flames. By placing the heads of this demon on her body Kali protects the world from destruction. The heads also represent men who have been sacrificed to her or who have sacrificed themselves to her. According to metaphysicians, the heads are symbols of the ego that must be offered to Kali by those seeking liberation from worldly ties. In the nationalistic discourse that saw Kali as Bharat Mata, these are the heads of martyrs. In the Tantrik tradition, each head represents a Sanskrit alphabet. Kali decapitates words so that the seeker of truth is liberated from the limitations imposed by language.

Kali also has a girdle of arms around her waist, probably a later-day addition by artists who found the nakedness of Kali too discomfiting. Metaphysicians view this as the bonds of karma that Kali cuts down, liberating her devotees from the cycle of rebirth. Nationalists saw them as the arms of those who laid their lives fighting for the liberation of the motherland.

The corpses of newborns serve as Kali's earrings. Kali thus becomes the explanation for the inexplicable deaths of newborns.

Nakedness

Kali is naked. Her nakedness represents Nature, unfettered by the norms of culture. Over the centuries, as Kali moved from the periphery of spiritual practices to the centre stage, from occult rituals to household ceremonies, artists have expressed their alarm at her immodesty in various ways. Most make sure that her hair and the garland of human heads and hands cover her sexual organs. Some have even bedecked her with ornaments of pearl and gold. In temples, one often finds her naked body adorned with a silk sari. The traditional offering in Devi shrines is a piece of cloth so that she can cover her nakedness and appear as a loving bride or a nourishing mother. Through this ritual the devotee expresses his desire to see the world not as a wild and untamed place but as a place where all emotions and actions are controlled by the law of civilization. The devotee seeks not the untamed forest but the domesticated field, he wants Devi not as the bloodthirsty Kali but as the milk-giving Gauri. The disrobing of Draupadi by the Kauravas in the Mahabharata is seen in the Tantrik tradition as an attempt to unravel the codes of civilization and the return of Devi into her wild, bloodthirsty state.

Body

In her earliest descriptions in the *Puranas*, Kali is described as gaunt with shrivelled breasts and sunken stomach or a potbelly. Later, especially in the *Tantras*, and with the rise of devotional movements, Kali came to be described as an extremely beautiful girl with full breasts and a narrow waist. In the former, no attempt is made to appeal to aesthetics of the observer. In the latter, the observer is expected to reconcile the gentleness of Kali's body with the brutality of her deeds.

Although Kali is considered the consort of Shiva and in many images is shown copulating with him, she is also, like most other goddesses, called the virgin. The idea of being a virgin indicates that the Devi, the ultimate Goddess, is subservient to no man. Nature is the supreme power, shedding and reclaiming its fertility at its own volition.

Four hands

In keeping with the Hindu tradition of depicting gods and goddesses with more heads and hands than ordinary human beings, Kali is shown in most works of art with four hands. Depending on the scripture and the form of Kali being worshipped, the hands bear a variety of weapons, including scimitar, sickle, scythe, sword, axe, trident or whip. The goddess also holds in one of her hands a freshly cut male head. The blood dripping from the severed neck is collected in a cup (usually the cranium of a skull). Some scriptures say that the cup contains wine, others say it contains the nectar of immortality. In household shrines, especially where Kali is called Dakshina-Kali or Bhadra-Kali, her hands take up the postures associated with protection and blessing known as *abhaya mudra* and *varada mudra*. Kali never holds in her hands symbols associated with fertility and fructification, such as sugarcane, parrot, flowers, conch shell and pot. These are associated with the benign and motherly aspect of Devi.

Posture

In most images, Kali appears to be walking from the south in the direction of the devotee, frozen momentarily when she accidentally steps on Shiva, with her left foot on his chest. Left is associated with feminine instinct while right is the side of masculine logic. Shiva thus restrains Kali's instinctive urge to be wild and free. Narratives inform us that this is essential for the sake of safegaurding culture. Otherwise, after killing demons and drinking their blood, Kali loses all control and kills randomly until Shiva intervenes.

In Tantrik texts, Shiva is not simply a physical obstacle. He waylays Kali with his handsome face and beautiful body, stirring her erotic urges until they overpower her violent side. Hence in Tantrik iconography, Kali does not merely sit on Shiva; she copulates with him while drinking blood from a human skull.

Sometimes Kali is depicted seated on a throne held up by male gods such as Indra, Brahma, Vishnu and Shiva. As Chamunda, she sits on a pile of corpses.

Surroundings

Kali always stands amidst death and decay. It is grey and gloomy around her. She is to be found in battlegrounds and cremation grounds. The battleground witnesses the collapse of culture and orderly conduct, giving way to unbridled violence as man lets loose his rage. The cremation ground witnesses the triumph of nature as death claims one and all.

Companions

Kali's male companions include Virabhadra or the eight Bhairavas who are the fierce manifestations of Shiva. They are variously described as her sons, husbands, brothers, priests and attendants. Kali is visualized either dancing with them, being adored by them, or standing or sitting on them.

Kali's female companions include hags (dakinis), witches (yoginis), mothers (matrikas) and virgins (kumaris). Either she is part of their collective or they stand around adoring her.

Cats are sacred to the Devi in general and Kali in particular. The Devi rides, hence domesticates, male cats. Harming female cats is supposed to incur her wrath. Male cats are known to kill their young so that the female cats stop nursing, come into heat rapidly and become receptive to their sexual demands. Female cats, on the other hand, protect their young fiercely, thus becoming the symbol of motherhood. In the *Devi Bhagvatam Purana* and the *Devi Bhagvatam,* Kali rides into battle on a lion. She thus domesticates even the lord of the jungle. In Punjab, Kali is sometimes addressed as 'Sheravali'—she of the tigers. In Tantrik art, black cats are closely associated with Kali. Occasionally, Kali is visualized riding, hence taming, a sexually aroused bull-elephant, otherwise considered to be unstoppable and dangerous. Thus Kali subdues even the most powerful beast's desire to dominate and have its way.

Kali also rides dogs, considered inauspicious, as they symbolize death. In the form of the gaunt Chamunda, Kali is associated with scorpions that have no utility, only a venomous sting and a legacy of ripping open their mothers' bellies during birth. They are all dear to Kali. In Kali's presence, even the most unappealing aspects of the cosmos reclaim their divinity.

All fertility goddesses, including Kali, are associated with snakes. Snakes are symbols of renewal—they shed their skin regularly and rejuvenate themselves just like the earth restores its fertility each year. Snakes are also symbols of kundalini, the seed of occult wisdom that lies coiled in all beings, waiting to be aroused by various Tantrik practices.

The Manifestations

Although today Kali is worshipped as an autonomous goddess manifesting in a variety of forms, in her long history she has been visualized as part of a divine female collective, as the embodiment of one of the three Devi powers, and as the 'other' face of the two-faced village-goddess. Over the centuries there has been a rise of several deities who display Kali-like characteristics but distinguish themselves from her in name and narrative. Much of the information about the manifestations of Kali comes to us from folklore and from the manuscripts known as *Tantras*, written after the sixth century AD.

One who takes many forms

According to *Mahanirvana Tantra*, Kali is adya, the primal form of the Devi, and the Maha-Vidyas are her emanations. *Naradapancharatra* mentions there are seven crore Maha-Vidyas and as many Upa-Vidyas; their number can never be settled conclusively. Thus Kali has innumerable forms and is known by many names. In the *Shakti-sangama Tantra*, according to Hadimata, one of the several contributors to the manuscript, Maha-Shakti is called Kali in Kerala, Tripura in Kashmira and Tara in Gauda (Bengal), while according to Kadimata, another contributor, she is called Tripura in Kerala, Tarini in Kashmira and Kali in Gaura. Kali has eight forms in *Todala-Tantra*: Dakshina-, Siddha-, Guhya-,

Shri-, Bhadra-, Chamunda-, Smashana- and Maha-Kali.
Mahakala Samhita enumerates nine types of Kali:
Dakshina-, Bhadra-, Smashana-, Kala-, Guhya-,
Kamakala-, Dhana-, Siddhi- and Chandika-Kali. The
tenth-century *Jayadhratayamala* mentions twelve forms
of Kali—Kalika, Dambara, Raksha, Indivara, Dhanda,
Ramani, Ishana, Jiva, Virya, Dhyana, Prajna and
Saptarna—each representing a state of consciousness,
with the highest state symbolized by the thirteenth Kali,
Kalasamkarshini.

Dakshina-Kali, enshrined in temples and even in
households, is the most important of Kali's forms
because it is her most acceptable and conventional form.
She is characterized by a fierce but smiling face, four
hands, untied hair and a garland of severed heads. She
is naked, dark, full breasted, holds a severed head in
one hand and a sword in the other. The third hand is
raised to protect while the fourth arm blesses. She steps
on a corpse-like Shiva as she approaches from the south.
The devotee considers her his mother.

Smashana-Kali is the form of Kali that is restricted
to the cremation ground. Unlike Dakshina-Kali who is
bluish purple in colour, she is black. She neither blesses,
nor gives boons. She looks fierce with snakes slithering
around her body and jackals keeping her company. She
drinks blood, yells into the night and dances with goblins.
The Tantrik aspirant seeks to face her without fear and

thus win her appreciation.

Siddha-Kali is the form taken by Kali when she is pleased with the Tantrik aspirant. In this form, she reveals the occult mysteries of the cosmos to the worthy hero and makes him powerful. Bejewelled with the sun and moon as her earrings, she has the complexion of a deep blue lotus in the moonlight. She has a flaming tongue and drinks the nectar of immortality from a skull, which she shares with the Tantrik hero.

Guhya-Kali, according to *Tantra Sara*, is the mysterious occult teacher of Tantra who lives in caves far away from human habitation. She has sunken eyes, wears black clothes, and has snakes for jewellery. Sometimes she has the crescent moon on her forehead, sometimes she nurses Shiva who takes the form of her child, and sometimes she appears with ten heads before those determined to see her.

As Bhadra-Kali, the fierce protector, she holds weapons of war in her hands, including an axe, a trident, a whip, a bell and a rattle-drum to frighten enemies. The skull that she uses as her drinking bowl also serves as the top of her mace.

As Chamunda-Kali, she is dark, emaciated, gaunt with bloodshot eyes, fangs and claws, shrivelled breasts, a scorpion on her sunken belly and a tiger skin around her waist. She sits on a pile of corpses, eats entrails, smears herself with gore, and drinks blood.

One of two

Traditionally, Tantrik schools are classified as Kali-*kula* and Shri-*kula*—the former worships the dark, fearsome forms of the Devi and the latter worships the fair, alluring forms. As Kali, the Devi is Tripura-Bhairavi, the most terrifying form in the three worlds; as Shri-Vidya, she is Tripura-Sundari, the most beautiful form. As Kali, the Devi bears weapons of war and skulls; as Shri, she bears symbols of fertility, including sugarcane, a parrot, conch shells and lotus flowers. As Kali, the Devi demands blood sacrifice; as Shri she gives food and knowledge to her devotees. Kali thus represents the 'other' face of Nature, one that is wild and untamed, one that is associated with death and decay, one that mankind tries very hard to deny, repress and suppress. Those of the Kali-*kula* school are also known as Vama-Tantriks or the left-handed Tantriks because their rites include objects and activities that defile the sanctity of religion, such as the use of flesh, alcohol, blood, corpses, hallucinogens and sex. Those of the Dakshina-Tantra or the right-handed Tantra school, who worship the Devi as Shri-Vidya, practise the same rites symbolically, substituting fruits and vegetables for animal and human sacrifices and red powder for blood.

The idea of the 'two-faced' goddess is at the core of the simplest and most ancient form of Devi-worship that exists in most villages of India, where a grama-devi or a village-goddess embodies the village itself. The deity is commonly represented by a vermillion- or saffron-smeared stone with a prominent pair of metal eyes. She has no body; the entire village—with its houses and fields—constitutes her body. The villagers in effect, live on the body of the village-goddess. This body is nothing but the wilderness, which has been fenced and domesticated to sustain a human settlement. Metaphorically speaking, wild Nature has been tamed, Kali has been converted to Shri, in order to establish and sustain the village.

However, once a year, the village-goddess returns to her wild state: Shri becomes Kali. Her tongue spreads across the village and she demands blood. This happens in autumn, after the harvest. This is the time when a male buffalo representing the dark, unspoken desires of the villagers—visualized as a demon—is sacrificed to the village-goddess. In the celebrations that follow, women get hysterical fits as they let their suppressed emotions express themselves. Men walk on fire or indulge in hook-swinging. Blood is spilt and pain experienced. The village experiences the wild side of Nature that the villagers otherwise keep at bay with their rules in order to establish and preserve the community.

Villagers address the grama-devi as Amma, Ai, Mata—various vernacular terms for mother. Her life-giving form Shri is known by various names, including Gauri, the radiant one; Mangala, the auspicious one; Bimala, the untainted one; and Lalita, the beautiful one. Her life-taking form Kali is known as Bhairavi, the fearsome one; Chamunda, the killer; Chandi, the aggressive one; and Jari-Mari, the hot-cold one. The following story from *Shiva Purana* clearly links the two forms of the Devi:

Kali's dark form, outstretched tongue, naked body scared everyone in the three worlds. The terrified gods, demons and humans invoked Shiva and begged him to calm her down. Shiva promised to help. He stood before Kali and began laughing. 'Why are you laughing?' asked a curious Kali. 'They say you are beautiful. But take a look at yourself; you look dark and hideous,' replied Shiva. Kali went to a river and saw her reflection. She realized what Shiva said was true. She bathed in the river until her black skin turned golden. She emerged looking beautiful. Shiva called her Gauri, the radiant one, and took her to his abode where she resumed her role as his consort. Kali's dark complexion was absorbed by the river, which became deep blue in colour. The river became known as Kalindi.

One of three

Between the fifth century BC and the fifth century AD, Hinduism was transformed. Vedic rituals were being abandoned, monastic ideology was gaining popularity and society was becoming increasingly theistic. People sought an almighty deity who answered their prayers and solved their problems. Some visualized the deity as male—either the ascetic Shiva or the regal Vishnu. Others visualized the deity as female.

Devi-worshippers were known as Shaktas. Their deity, Mahadevi (which literally means 'the great goddess') was the embodiment of shakti (energy or substance of the cosmos), prakriti (the natural, material world), and maya (perceived reality). In shrines, she was represented by three stones, each stone embodying a third of her divinity. The stones represented Maha-Lakshmi, Maha-Saraswati, and Maha-Kali, the goddesses of wealth, knowledge and power. Shrines where three stones still represent the Devi are located at Vaishno-Devi in Jammu, Mookambika in Karnataka and Maha-Lakshmi in Mumbai.

As one of the triad, Kali is rarely depicted with an outstretched tongue, but her symbols such as the lion and the trident dominate the shrine. Blood sacrifice associated with Kali is, however, discouraged as worshippers prefer to visualize the goddess in her milder, vegetarian form.

The following story from a Kannada ballad, which is a recurring theme in many folk narratives, informs us how the three forms of the Devi came into being when male deities usurped the primal position once occupied by the ultimate female divinity. In the story, cultural values such as incest taboo are associated with the male deities, implying that the female deities are embodiments of 'wild Nature' while the male deities are upholders of 'domesticated Culture':

Once long ago, even before there was the sun and the moon in the sky, there bloomed a lotus in the ocean of milk. On that lotus sat the Goddess, Mahadevi, who is Adi-Maya-Shakti, the mother of all forms. All alone and lonely, she decided to create a consort to please her. She produced three eggs. From the first one came Brahma, who looked like a priest ready to perform a *yagna*. From the second came Vishnu, who looked like a king ready to uphold *dharma*. From the third came Shiva, with matted locks, who looked like an ascetic. All three were handsome and the Devi desired them all. She first went to Brahma. 'Be my husband and make me happy,' she said, smiling coquettishly. Brahma was horrified. 'You are my mother,' he said, 'You ask me to do what a son must not do!' Mahadevi said, 'This does not apply to me. I make the rules.' Brahma refused to satisfy the Devi. Angry, she opened her third eye, let loose a glance of fire and reduced Brahma to ashes. The Devi then approached Vishnu. He too turned away, refusing to do what a son must not do with his mother. His fate was the same as Brahma's. Then standing between two piles of ashes where Brahma and Vishnu once stood, Mahadevi looked at Shiva. 'Well, will you be my husband and quench my thirst?' Shiva knew what was in store for him if he refused. 'I will,' he said, 'But don't you think to be a worthy husband I should have more strength than you? Otherwise everyone will mock you and me.' The Devi agreed. She shared her wisdom with Shiva, even the ability to create things out of thin air. But Shiva was not satisfied. Give me the jewel that rests on your forehead. 'That is no jewel. That is the third eye, the source of all my power,' said Mahadevi. 'Give me the third eye, then,' said Shiva. Mahadevi, blinded by lust, agreed. She plucked out her third eye and gave it to Shiva. No sooner had he laid his hands on the Devi's power than he reduced her to ashes. Then using his new-found powers, Shiva revived

Brahma and Vishnu. They looked at the heap of ash where Mahadevi once stood. 'What do we do with that?' They decided to create wives out of it. They divided the ash into three heaps. Brahma transformed one heap into Lakshmi, made her the goddess of wealth, called her his sister and gave her in marriage to Vishnu. Vishnu transformed the second heap into Kali, made her the goddess of power, called her his sister and gave her in marriage to Shiva. Shiva transformed the third heap into Saraswati, made her the goddess of knowledge, called her his sister and gave her in marriage to Brahma. From the tiny amounts of ash left behind came many dark, naked and fierce-looking goddesses with fangs, bloodshot eyes and unbound hair, holding serpents and sickles in their hands. These became village-goddesses, ready to fight with demons and inflict disease on villagers who annoyed them.

One of several

Kali or a Kali-like goddess is often one of the seven Kumaris (virgins), one of the seven Matrikas (mothers), one of the ten Maha-Vidyas (teachers), one of the sixty-four Yoginis (witches) or one of the 108 Dakinis (crones). Although each member of these groups has a unique name and a characteristic form, no member is worshipped in isolation. They are sacred as a group.

The Matrikas are no different from Kumaris—virgins who inadvertently become the mothers of Skanda, the hypermasculine commander of the celestial armies. Skanda is born of the seed of one god—Agni, the fire-god, in early scriptures, and Shiva, the ascetic-god, in later scriptures—which is so potent that it needs to be incubated in seven virgin wombs. The narratives vary on how the seven sisters, sometimes described as wives of the seven celestial sages, get pregnant. In the following story from the Mahabharata, the sisters make love to Agni through a surrogate:

> The fire-god, Agni, burnt with lust at the sight of the wives of the seven celestial sages but he knew that his passion for married women was inappropriate. He would caress the women with his heat and light each time they approached the fire-altar to make offerings to the gods. Realizing that it was just a matter of time before Agni had illicit relations with these unsuspecting women, Agni's consort Svaha decided to take the matter into her own hands. She took the form of the seven women and made love to her husband seven times. She succeeded only six times as the seventh sister was too chaste. Agni

therefore spilt his seed six times. This Svaha collected and transformed into a single hypermasculine child called Skanda who was powerful enough to lead the celestial armies even when he was a child. His passion spent, Agni thanked Svaha for saving him from committing an unforgivable crime.

In the *Skanda Purana*, six of them become pregnant when they bathe in a pond in which the gods have placed a potent seed of Shiva. Though innocent, the women are accused of adultery. To purify their bodies of shame, they shed the unborn child. A forest fire fuses the six foetuses into the six-headed Skanda. The virgins are sometimes called the Krittikas, hence Skanda is also known as Kartikeya, the son of the six virgins.

The Mahabharata mentions that outraged at being penalized for no fault of theirs, the virgins turn into ferocious beings. They decide to kill Skanda, but no sooner do they lay their eyes on their child than they are overcome with maternal affection. Skanda declares, 'If women do not worship you, feel free to destroy their unborn and newborn children.' The virgins thus became goddesses of several childhood ailments. They are appeased with offerings of neem leaves, curd and lemons every time a child or pregnant woman has fever with pox or rashes. Their shrines are no more than seven vermillion-smeared stones on the banks of water bodies, usually under neem trees.

In later sculptures, written after the tenth century AD, the seven mothers are visualized as the female forms of seven popular Hindu gods: Shiva, Vishnu, Brahma, Narasimha, Varaha, Kumara and Indra. Sometimes, the goddess Chamunda is listed amongst them. Chamunda with her gaunt features, nakedness and bloodlust is said to be a form of Kali.

Like the Matrikas, the Maha-Vidyas and the Yoginis too appear in narratives as manifestations of outrage. Some of them have the form of Kali. The Maha-Vidyas first appear when Sati decides to disrupt her father's *yagna*, intended to insult her hermit-husband Shiva. The Yoginis appear when Parvati threatens to destroy the world unless her son Vinayaka, who has been beheaded by Shiva, is restored to life.

A careful observation of these groups shows that they signify the various reactions Nature has evoked in man. Nature can be anything from the wild and terrifying to the tame and beautiful. Kali embodies the wild side with her nakedness and bloodlust, while Kamala embodies the gentle side with her bejewelled form and lotus seat. Often these collective goddesses have one male form beside them, either Skanda or Ganesha, or more commonly, Bhairava—the fierce form of Shiva. The male form is described variously as the attendant, priest, brother, son or consort of the divine female collective.

Almost Kali

Across India we find many Kali-like goddesses. Prominent among these are Chamunda, Alakshmi, Bhagavati, Chinnamastika, and Tara. They probably originated from the same primordial cultural substratum from where all forms of the Devi emerged.

Most devotees do not distinguish between Chamunda and Kali. In some scriptures Chamunda is clearly identified as a form of Kali. Their identities often coalesce because they are dark, naked, wild and bloodthirsty. But there are differences. Chamunda is emaciated and ugly while Kali is dishevelled but beautiful. Chamunda sits on a pile of corpses while Kali stands on Shiva. Unlike Kali, Chamunda does not stretch out her tongue. Chamunda rides ghosts and has scorpions on her body, while Kali rides lions, and sometimes elephants. Chamunda is associated more with death and decay while Kali is associated more with unbridled sex and violence.

Alakshmi, the goddess of misfortune, is the sister of Lakshmi, the goddess of fortune. Together they constitute the totality of the Devi. While in Tantra the inauspicious form of the Devi is worshipped, in Vaishnavism—strictly a religion of householders—

preference is given only to the auspicious forms. Thus, in Vaishnava rituals, Lakshmi is worshipped as the consort of Vishnu who is the upholder of social values and worldly order, while Alakshmi is driven away as she embodies all things that threaten civilization—dirt, pollution, gluttony, sloth, greed, envy, hunger, disease and war. While Lakshmi sits bejewelled on a lotus holding a pot, Alakshmi wears torn clothes, rides a donkey and carries a broom. Lakshmi is offered sweets and kept inside the house; Alakshmi is offered lemons and chillies and thrown out of the house. The following story illustrates the conventional attitude towards Alakshmi:

Lakshmi and Alakshmi, the goddesses of fortune and misfortune respectively, once went to a merchant and asked him who was more beautiful of the two. The merchant knew the price of annoying either one. So he came up with a very clever answer. He said, 'Lakshmi is beautiful when she walks into the house while Alakshmi is beautiful when she leaves the house.' Immediately, Lakshmi walked towards the merchant's house while Alakshmi walked away from it. Consequently, the merchant was visited by fortune while misfortune stayed away, much to the merchant's delight.

Bhagavati is one of the most popular 'hot' goddesses of Kerala. In the ritual art of Teyyam, she is invoked through oracles and through the dancers who go in a trance as soon as she 'enters' their bodies and begins to 'speak' through their tongues. Usually the goddess has no permanent shrine dedicated to her. Devotees create her image on the floor using coloured powder on festival days, which is wiped out at the end of the ceremony. The goddess looks ferocious with bloodshot eyes, fangs and clawed fingers. She demands offerings, usually chickens and goats, from villagers before promising them peace and prosperity. Sometimes songs with obscene lyrics describing her insatiable sexual cravings are sung to amuse this virgin goddess, although this practice is now on the wane. In narratives it is said that this goddess was first invoked to kill a demon. Every year after this demon is ritually killed—either in song or through sacrifice—Bhagavati leaves the body of the oracle or the dancer. The devotees who invoked her return to their daily routine, safe in the knowledge that Bhagavati is happy and will take care of them until her return the following year.

Chinnamastika, like Kali, is one of the Maha-Vidyas—teachers of occult wisdom. Chinnamastika is described as a naked goddess who cuts her own head and drinks the blood that spurts out of her severed neck while either copulating with Shiva or dancing on a couple making love. The image brings together acts of sex, violence, defence and nourishment. Chinnamastika reconciles the creative and destructive sides of the cosmos as she feeds on what she kills. She embodies the stark reality of Nature that culture shies away from. Her image is never enshrined in households because it appeals more to the Tantrik aspirant who has broken free from the restrictions imposed by civilized society and who is willing to explore those aspects of the universe that society deems inappropriate and inauspicious.

In Bengal, Tara is another name for Kali, although the two are treated as two distinct goddesses in the list of Maha-Vidyas. In Tibet, Tara is the name of a goddess who is quite unlike her Bengali namesake. The Tibetan Tara is described as a gentle and charming goddess who holds a lotus in her hand. She was born from the tear of compassion shed by the Bodhisattva Avatilokeshwara when he heard the cries of those trapped in the cycle of rebirths. The link between the Tibetan Tara and the Bengali Tara has perhaps much to do with the religious communication that existed for centuries between Bengal and Tibet.

In Tibetan Tantrik Buddhism, a goddess who is more like Kali, at least in form, is Nairatma ('no soul') —the consort of Heruka. Her name means shunya or 'nothingness' into which the Bodhichitta, the enlightened soul, merges on attaining Nirvana. That is why she is represented in eternal union with her consort.

Individually she is represented as standing in a dancing mode on a corpse. Her face looks terrible with bare and protruding tongue and she carries a kartari (dagger) in her right hand and kapala (skull-bowl) in the left, just like Kali.

The Tales

Stories help establish the character of Hindu deities. These stories are found in epics such as the Ramayana and the Mahabharata and in chronicles such as the *Puranas*. Some are retold in the *Tantras* and *Agamas*, others are found in folklore. These stories reach the common man through vernacular retellings. Each retelling has a character of its own.

Over the centuries, there have been many retellings of Kali's tale. These have portrayed her in a variety of forms. In some, she is the manifestation of divine outrage. In others, she is the final defender of the cosmos to whom the gods turn when all measures fail. She is the goddess who demands human sacrifice. She represents all that is wild and untamed in the universe. Without her, even God is inert and lifeless.

It must be kept in mind that while in some stories Kali's unique identity in the pantheon of gods and goddesses is established, in others she is merely a name used to refer to the female divinity. In other words, in some stories there is a clear relationship between the narrative and her characteristic form while in others, the narrative is totally indifferent to her form.

Manifestation of divine rage

One of the earliest stories where Kali plays a central role is found in the *Devi Mahatmya*, where Kali appears as the embodiment of Durga's rage when she loses her composure.

The gods once gathered on the banks of the river Ganga to invoke the Devi and seek her help to overpower two demons known as Shumbha and Nishumbha. Parvati, consort of the hermit-god Shiva, who happened to be passing by heard their prayer. Instantly a goddess emerged from her body. Since she emerged from the koshas or cells of Parvati's body, she became known as Kaushiki. As she looked like a warrior, quite unlike the docile and domestic Parvati, she was also known as Chandika. Chandika was very beautiful, so she was also called Lalita and Vimala. News of her beauty reached Shumbha and Nishumbha. Desirous of making her their queen, the demons sent her a marriage proposal. To their surprise she sent the following reply: 'I shall accept as husband only the man who defeats me in battle.' Infuriated by this open challenge, Shumbha and Nishumbha ordered their minions, Chanda and Munda, to bring Chandika before them by force. 'Bind her and drag her by the hair if she resists,' they said. Chanda and Munda raised an army and found Chandika atop Mount

Meru. She sat on a lion and was smiling to herself. At the sight of the demons, Chandika's face blackened with anger and from her dark frowning brow emerged Kali—dark, gaunt, with bloodshot eyes, sharp fangs and lolling tongue. She let out a shrill war-cry and rushed towards Chanda and Munda. The demon army raised their bows but before they could shoot a single arrow, Kali was upon them. She broke their bows, hurled aside their chariots and devoured their elephants. There was havoc all around Chanda and Munda. Kali disembowelled a few demons with her bare hands, others she chewed alive with her fangs, earning the title of Raktadantika, the red-toothed one. The rest she crushed under her feet. Finally Kali came face to face with Chanda and Munda. With a single swipe of her sword she beheaded both of them. She gifted their heads to Chandika who declared that as killer of Chanda and Munda, Kali would be known as Chamunda. In due course, after a great battle, Chandika overpowered Shumbha and Nishumbha and restored order in the world. To celebrate this victory, the gods composed the hymn known as Chandi-patha, the 'call to the warrior goddess'.

Kali who personifies wrath also appears as alter-ego of the gentle mountain-princess Parvati, consort of the ascetic-god Shiva, in the *Skanda Purana,* composed around the eleventh century.

Daksha was the son of Brahma and the supreme patriarch of the Vedic way of life. He had given his daughters in marriage to the devas, Vedic gods who inhabit the celestial spheres. Much to his consternation, his youngest daughter, Sati, rejected the deva chosen for her and married Shiva instead. Shiva was an ascetic who meditated in isolation atop the snow-capped Himalayas. He did not respect the Vedic ways, and gave no importance either to the ritual known as yagna or its principal patron, Daksha. Piqued by Shiva's refusal to grant him due respect, Daksha decided to perform a grand yagna. All the devas were invited to take a share of the offerings but no invitation was extended to Shiva. When Sati learnt of this, she was furious. She decided to go to her father's house uninvited and demand an explanation. Shiva tried to dissuade her but she refused to listen to him. When he tried to stop her by force she rubbed her nose in anger and filled the ten directions with ten furious forms—the Maha-

Vidyas—the first of which was Kali. Shiva, thus terrified, let Sati attend the ceremony.

In the *Shiva Purana*, composed at least six centuries before the *Skanda Purana*, one finds the same narrative. But there, Kali is a manifestation of Shiva's, not Sati's, rage.

Sati strode into her father's house and immolated herself in the sacred pavilion to protest against Shiva's exclusion from the yagna. Daksha, however, continued with the ceremony. When news of Sati's death and Daksha's indifference reached Shiva, he was so furious that he plucked a lock of his hair and lashed it against the ground to create an army of demonic beings led by the fierce-looking warrior Virabhadra and his equally ferocious companion, the goddess Bhadra-Kali. Virabhadra and Bhadra-Kali rushed into Daksha's house and set about disrupting the ritual. They kicked the sacred vessels, spat on the offerings, attacked the assembled guests, scared away the gods, and finally beheaded Daksha.

Rural India is full of village-goddesses or grama-devis who are often addressed or visualized as Kali.

Songs and stories about these goddesses invariably speak of some tragedy that befalls a village woman, who then transforms herself into a goddess. It is clear from these narratives that the grama-devis embody female frustration and helpless rage. In the form of the terrifying Kali, this repressed anger haunts the collective subconscious of the village, demanding appeasement and retribution. The earliest documented tale of this genre comes from the fifth-century Tamil epic, *Cilappatikaram*.

Kannagi's husband, Kovalan, a merchant by profession, squandered his family fortune on a courtesan named Madhavi. Everyone, except his devoted wife, abandoned him in his hour of need. Realizing his folly, he decided to move to the city of Madurai and start life afresh. To help him raise capital for his new venture, Kannagi agreed to let Kovalan sell one of her gold anklets. Unfortunately, the gold anklet looked very much like the anklet of the queen of Madurai and the unscrupulous goldsmiths accused Kovalan of theft. The king, without bothering to check the facts, ordered that Kovalan be impaled to death. When news of Kovalan's death reached Kannagi she was heartbroken. After the sorrow came the rage. She strode into the king's court with the second anklet and demanded justice. The king apologized but Kannagi could not find it in her heart to forgive. So great was the widow's fury that she plucked her breasts and hurled them in the city square. Instantly the city burst into flames. All its residents, including the goldsmiths and the king, were reduced to ashes. Kannagi emerged from the flames as a goddess called Pattini, the chaste one.

Pattini is worshipped in parts of Tamil Nadu, Kerala and even Sri Lanka as a form of Bhadra-Kali. The ferocious form of the goddess is viewed as a manifestation of her righteous outrage.

In many parts of India, the grama-devi is known as Mari-Amma or Mari-Ai. She is believed to be a local manifestation of Maha-Kali, who appeared when she discovered that her husband had cheated her. The following story is a folk narrative, popular in villages of Andhra Pradesh and Karnataka.

Once there lived a woman, a Brahmin's daughter, who believed she had married a learned Brahmin scholar. But one day, she heard his mother telling him, 'It has been a long time since we ate some beef.' She realized instantly that her husband was no Brahmin; he was a low-caste beef-eater.

Enraged at being duped, she transformed herself into Maha-Kali. She decapitated her husband and set fire to her house, burning her mother-in-law, her children and herself in it.

In Gujarat, Maha-Kali is the name of Bahucharji Mata, the goddess of hijras or eunuchs, who presides over their castration ritual. She is visualized as riding a rooster. Her tale informs us of her rage when she discovered that her husband was not capable of satisfying her sexual desires.

Final defender

The *Devi Mahatmya* also presents Kali as the ultimate deliverer called upon to salvage a situation that seems hopelessly out of control. She is summoned by Durga herself to destroy the demon Rakta-bija, whose name means 'blood-seed'.

The demon Rakta-bija had the magical ability to produce a clone of himself every time a drop of his blood fell to the ground. Having wounded Rakta-bija with a variety of weapons, Durga and her assistants—a fierce band of warriors known as the Matrikas—find they have only aggravated the situation: as Rakta-bija bleeds more and more profusely from his wounds, the battlefield increasingly becomes filled with replicas of Rakta-bija. Desperate, Durga summons Kali. Kali spreads her tongue across the battlefield, swallows in one gulp the swarm of blood-born demons and sucks the blood from the original Rakta-bija until he falls lifeless.

In the Sanskrit *Adbhuta Ramayana* and *Devi Bhagvata Purana,* in the Oriya *Ramayana* of Sarala Das, and in the Bengali *Jaminibharata Ramayana*, Sita takes the form of Kali to defeat the demon who even Rama, the earthly form of Vishnu, cannot vanquish.

After killing the ten-headed demon-king of Lanka called Ravana who had abducted his wife Sita, Rama returned to Ayodhya and was crowned king. His subjects, however, were uncomfortable accepting Sita as they suspected that her association with Ravana had stained her reputation. Yielding to their demands, Rama abandoned Sita in the forest where she gave birth to Rama's twin sons: Luv and Kush. Meanwhile, far away in Lanka, one of Ravana's widows gave birth to Ravana's son: a demon called Sahashra-mukha-Ravana, 'the-thousand-headed-Ravana'. This demon was determined to avenge his father's death. So he launched an attack on Ayodhya. Neither Rama nor his armies could vanquish this demon. When Rama learnt that this demon could only be defeated by the powers of a chaste woman, he requested the women of Ayodhya to fight Sahashra-mukha-Ravana. It became obvious to all that no woman in the city possessed enough chastity to overpower the demon. Desperate, Rama sent for Sita. At first she refused to come. So she was told a lie, that Rama was dying. Sita came rushing to be by her husband's side. On the way to Ayodhya she came upon Sahashra-mukha-Ravana who tried to block her way. Furious, Sita turned into Kali, raised the weapon containing the power of the Devi and cut all his hundred heads.

Once when the gods could not defeat the demon Daruka, they approached the ascetic-god Shiva who in turn turned to his wife Parvati. She was able to defeat Daruka but only after transforming herself into Kali. The following story forms the theme of many Malayali ballads sung while invoking Bhagavati in villages across Kerala.

Long ago, the gods and demons had churned the ocean of milk until it yielded Amrit—the nectar of immortality. Along with Amrit had come Halahal—the most dreaded poison. While gods and demons fought over Amrit, only Shiva was willing to consume Halahal and keep it in his throat so that it harmed no one. Halahal made Shiva's fair neck blue and so Shiva came to be known as Nila-kantha, the blue-necked god. Once, the gods were harassed by a demon called Daruka. They sang the Chandi-patha and begged the Devi to come to their rescue. Parvati heard their prayers and submerged herself in the poison locked in Shiva's throat. She emerged as Kali—as dark as the poison itself and much more lethal. The poison made Kali's body hot. She sought blood to quench her thirst. So she gnashed her teeth and ran after Daruka. She caught up with him and wrenched off his head with her bare hands. After drinking his blood, she tossed his head in the air and bedecked herself with his arms, legs and entrails.

Stories where Kali manifests as the final defender clearly establish the supremacy of the Devi, especially Kali, over other gods, including Vishnu and Shiva. Narratives of such kind became more frequent from the third to the thirteenth century when devotion to a personal god became the dominant form of religious expression. Worshippers of different deities tried to project their god as greater than other forms. Worshippers of Vishnu made Vishnu and his incarnations the most powerful manifestation of the divine, while worshippers of Shiva preferred Shiva or his son, Skanda, in the role of the supreme defender of the cosmos. In the scriptures of the goddess-worshippers, Durga, in her many manifestations, including Kali, emerges as the final deliverer in the battlefield.

Traditionally, the responsibility of maintaining order resides with Vishnu who descends on earth as Rama or Krishna to re-establish social stability. In the following story, told in one of the lesser-known *Upa-Puranas* of Bengal, Krishna is said to be none other than Kali, while Shiva lying at the feet of Kali becomes Radha. The narrative links the dark-complexioned god (Kali) of one narrative with the dark-complexioned god (Krishna) of another and reverses the sexual relationship with their fair-complexioned counterparts (Shiva/ Radha). This narrative was clearly aimed to harmonize relationship between the Tantrik rituals performed for Kali and the rites observed for Krishna in the Vaishnav tradition that vied for social domination in the seventeenth-century Bengal.

The gods begged Kali to rid the world of demonic kings. She agreed to become incarnate as Krishna. Shiva prayed to Kali and was given permission to incarnate on earth as Radha. Shiva had always been at the foot of Kali, but when he became Radha, he sat on top of Krishna/Kali while making love. So it came to pass that he who was at the bottom came to enjoy intercourse by being on top, but only after acquiring the body of a woman. While she who was on top came to enjoy intercourse by being at the bottom, but only after acquiring the body of a man.

The blood-thirsty goddess

In the *Bhagavata Purana*, the earth takes the form of a cow and complains to Vishnu, her celestial guardian, that kings who were supposed to take care of her plunder her resources. Vishnu promises to destroy all those who trouble the earth. He appears in various forms, including Parashurama, Rama and Krishna, and kills the unrighteous kings. As they fall, their blood nourishes the starving earth. The earth-goddess as the drinker of blood takes the form of lion—the vehicle of Kali. The story of Rakta-bija in the *Devi Bhagavatam*, retold earlier, also links Kali with a taste for blood.

Most classical narratives suggest the idea that the earth gives life only when the Devi is nourished by death, hence blood. In folk narratives, the idea is expressed more explicitly as in the mythology of North Tamil Nadu, where Draupadi of the Mahabharata is worshipped as the goddess Vira-Panchali, a form of Maha-Kali. The local lore informs us that Draupadi's rage at being publicly disrobed by the Kauravas while her five husbands, the Pandavas, watched helplessly transforms her into the terrifying goddess, Vira-Panchali. With the help of Krishna, the benefactor of the Pandavas, she not only ensures the defeat of the Kauravas, but also washes her hair with their blood. The following story is part of the folk Mahabharata retold in festivals of Vira-Panchali in parts of Tamil Nadu and Andhra Pradesh.

The Pandavas gambled away their kingdom to their cousins, the Kauravas, in a game of dice. In a bid to recover the kingdom the Pandavas staked themselves, but lost. Finally, desperate to recover their kingdom and their freedom, the Pandavas staked their common wife, Draupadi. They lost her too. The Kauravas dragged Draupadi by her hair into the court and began disrobing her in public to proclaim their absolute power over the Pandavas. Draupadi's cries for help fell on deaf ears. Helpless, she cried out to Krishna, who protected her honour by replacing every robe removed by the Kauravas with a fresh one. Realizing God was on Draupadi's side, the Kauravas decided to return the Pandavas their kingdom but only after a period of thirteen years during which they and their common wife were expected to live as exiles in the forest. The Pandavas accepted this offer. However, before they set out for the forest, Draupadi took an oath: she would leave her hair unbound until she had the blood of the Kauravas to wash her hair, the bones of the Kauravas to comb her hair, and the entrails of the Kauravas to tie her hair. During the years of exile, the Pandavas wondered why neither of them could satisfy Draupadi sexually. Krishna informed them that she was no ordinary woman; she was the Devi herself, the embodiment of Nature. By disrobing her, the Kauravas had caused her to shed her domesticated maternal form and reclaim her wild, bloodthirsty form. To convince them, Krishna suggested they observe Draupadi at night. Sure enough, at midnight, the hour when everyone was supposed to be asleep, Draupadi silently crept out into the forest where she transformed herself into a dark, naked, fierce-looking goddess with fangs and bloodshot eyes. She ran naked, hunting wild buffaloes and elephants, flaying them alive and drinking their blood. When she sensed that her husbands had discovered her secret, she was angry. She ran after them, determined to eat them. She would have succeeded, but as she grabbed them, her sharp nails cut their skin and caused them to bleed. When the blood of the five Pandavas touched the ground, they transformed into five children. The cries of the children diverted Draupadi's attention. She forgot her bloodlust and indulged her maternal instincts. Thirteen years later, when the Kauravas refused to return the Pandava kingdom as promised, a great war broke out in the plains of Kurukshetra where they were defeated and killed. The Pandavas were able to provide Draupadi with all the blood, bones and entrails she needed to bind her hair and become the loving queen once more.

The folk Mahabharata of the Tamils has another story where by offering blood to Kali the Pandavas ensure their victory in battle.

Krishna told the Pandavas that only the perfect human sacrifice would please Kali enough to assure them victory in battle. There were three men in the Pandava camp who were suitable victims: Krishna, Arjuna and Arjuna's son Aravan. The Pandavas were unwilling to sacrifice Krishna, their mentor, or Arjuna, their chief archer. Aravan agreed to be sacrificed but only if he had experienced conjugal bliss for at least a night. No woman was ready to marry a man doomed to die within a day. So Krishna took the form of a woman, the enchantress Mohini, who married Aravan, spent one night with him and mourned for him like a widow at dawn when he was sacrificed to Kali.

As Kali increasingly became assimilated into mainstream religion, she turned more 'righteous'. She did not accept the sacrifice of innocents as the following story from the *Bhagavata Purana* informs us.

The leader of a band of thieves was told that he would get a son if he sacrificed a Brahmin youth who had no blemish on his body to Kali. The thieves scoured the countryside and found such a youth. His name was Bharata, a devotee of Vishnu-Narayana, who was so absorbed in devotion that he never spoke and did his duties quietly. The thieves found him as he watched over his father's fields. They kidnapped him, gave him a bath and a good meal. Then smearing him with turmeric and vermillion, they took him before the image of Kali. As the priest prepared to sacrifice Bharata, something amazing happened. Bharata's body began to glow with his spiritual radiance. This radiance was too much for Kali to bear. She emerged from her idol and began devouring the thieves who sought to offer this lad to her. After quenching her thirst with the blood of the thieves she blessed Bharata and disappeared.

The preferred sacrifice was offering one's own self. In many images carved in temples of Kali, one sees devotees offering their own heads to the goddess as a sign of ultimate devotion. According to folklore, the poet Kalidasa, whose name means 'servant of Kali', acquired his talent after offering his head to the goddess Kali.

Kalidasa was a simpleton whose wife could not tolerate him. Determined to win her affection he invoked Kali by offering her his own head (or tongue) as sacrifice. The goddess was so pleased that she restored Kalidasa to life. She then swallowed him whole and vomited him out. By entering the body of the goddess, Kalidasa was cleansed of all stupidity. He emerged as a talented poet. No sooner was he reborn from the mouth of Kali he began composing a hymn in praise of the goddess. But instead of describing the goddess, who was now his mother, from the feet up, he began describing her from the face down. This act of disrespect infuriated Kali who declared that Kalidasa would die at the hands of a woman.

Taming the goddess

When Kali consumes blood, she is driven mad with bloodlust. She becomes wild and kills randomly. When this happens, the gods call upon Shiva and beg him to tame her. For, only in her tamed form can she be mother. According to a Tamil temple lore, this is how Shiva responds:

After defeating the demons and drinking their blood, Kali could not contain her rage. She continued killing and destroying everything in her path. The stability of the three worlds was at stake. So the gods along with Brahma and Vishnu begged Shiva to stop her. Shiva blocked Kali's march and challenged her to a dance competition. 'If you can outdo me in dance then you can behead me too,' he said. Kali took up the challenge and redirected her rage and passion from war into dance. The gods watched as Shiva and Kali danced. The earth trembled at they stamped their feet. The sun and moon hid behind the hills as the divine couple moved their hands. The dance continued for eons. Both dancers were equally matched. Kali could do whatever Shiva did. Shiva could do whatever Kali did. Neither could dominate the other. Then, suddenly, Shiva raised his left leg so that his left knee was behind his left ear and his left foot was over his head. Kali was about to raise her leg when she restrained herself out of feminine modesty. How could she take such a stance without exposing her privates to the whole world? She smiled shyly and accepted defeat. The gods saluted Shiva as Nataraja, the lord of dance. The position he took became renowned as Urdhva-Nataraja, the posture with upraised leg, that domesticated the wild Parvati.

This tale clearly attempts to resolve the conflict between the traditional role of women as being subservient to man and the symbolic role of women as the manifestation of the divine. As Kali increasingly became accepted as a deity of the mainstream religion, her independence began to threaten social stability that relied heavily on male domination. Narratives came to be woven which established that no matter how powerful the Devi was, she still remained subservient to the male form of the divine. In the following tale, for example, Kali is shamed into submission. The narrative, which has no scriptural foundation, explains Kali's most popular image where she sticks out her tongue.

> After killing the demon Daruka, Kali drank his blood. The blood drove her mad with bloodlust. She went around the world killing at random. The gods begged Shiva to stop her. So he took the form of a handsome man and lay in Kali's path. As soon as Kali stepped on him, she bit her tongue in embarrassment. She was ashamed to learn that her bloodlust had prevented her from seeing and recognizing her own husband.

In Tantrik narratives on the other hand, Kali neither sticks out her tongue in shame or embarrassment nor steps on Shiva accidentally. She sticks out her tongue to drink blood. And she sits on him to satisfy her erotic desires aroused by his beautiful form. Kali, in these narratives, is neither defensive nor apologetic about her hunger or her sexual cravings.

> After killing the demon Daruka, Kali drank his blood. The blood drove her mad with bloodlust. She went around the world killing at random. The gods begged Shiva to stop her. So he took the form of a handsome man and lay in Kali's path. As soon as Kali stepped on him, she was

overcome with desire. She sat on Shiva and began making love to him. Her violent energy was transformed into erotic energy. Her heat, which was destructive, became creative. She was no longer a killer; she was a lover.

The idea of Kali copulating in the open, sitting on top of her husband did not appeal to popular imagination, which was dominated by patriarchal values. A more acceptable form of the narrative is retold in the *Linga Purana*.

After killing the demon Daruka, Kali drank his blood. The blood drove her mad with bloodlust. She went around the world killing at random. The gods begged Shiva to stop her. So he took the form of a little baby and began to cry. As soon as Kali heard the cry, she was filled with motherly affection. Her breasts became full of milk and she was filled with an overwhelming desire to nurse the child. She picked up the baby and took care of it. Thus Shiva transformed her violent energy into productive energy. Her heat, which was destructive, became creative. She was no longer a killer; she was a mother.

Arousing God

Just as God tames the Devi, so does the Devi arouse God. While he may bridle her passion, she stirs his desire. Thus the two forms of the divine complement each other. In the following narrative from the *Shiva Purana*, the Devi forces the hermit Shiva to become a householder and father a child.

The demon Taraka terrorized the three worlds. Only a six-day-old child could kill him. The gods wondered where they could find a child who could go to battle on the seventh day of his life. Brahma informed them that only the ascetic Shiva was potent enough to father such a child. But for eons Shiva had shut his eyes and plunged himself in meditation. To rouse the lone ascetic, the gods sent Kandarpa, the love-god. When the love-god shot five arrows to rouse the five senses of Shiva, Shiva opened his third eye, let loose a fiery missile and reduced Kandarpa to ashes. Terrified of Shiva's power, the gods turned to the Devi. If anyone could make Shiva father a child, she could. The Devi took the form of Parvati, the mountain-princess, and served Shiva dutifully in the hope that he would eventually fall in love with her. It did not work. So she began performing austerities matching those of Shiva in intensity. So intense was her meditation that the earth shook from its very foundation. Shiva had no choice but to open his eyes and agree to marry her. Thus domesticated, Shiva made love to his consort Parvati. He eventually shed his semen that was so potent that it started fire, brought rivers to boil and set forests ablaze. Finally the seed transformed into the six-headed boy-god Skanda, who on the seventh day of his life took command of celestial armies, launched an attack against Taraka, and killed him in battle.

In the *Purana*, the Devi 'marries' Shiva and ensures he becomes worldly. But in the *Tantra*, this idea is expressed more explicitly. Shiva is visualized as so absorbed in meditation that he senses nothing of the outside world; he is like a corpse. None approaches him fearing his wrath, lest he be disturbed. Kali not only walks up to Shiva, she sits on him and forces him to copulate with her. She thus stirs Shiva's mind and forces him to acknowledge the external material world. This has led to the following statement in the *Todala Tantra*: 'Sadashiva is without energy (lifeless) unless Maha-Kali is manifest. He also is like a corpse (shava) without union with Shakti. Clearly, without Shakti, the primordial god is lifeless and cannot act.'

In Hindu metaphysics, God is the spiritual principle and the Devi is the material principle. He is the spirit, she is the substance. He is the cause, she is the manifestation. He is the divine within, she is the divine without. He gives her form, she gives him meaning. One cannot exist without the other. If Shiva is kala or time, then Kali is the force that rotates it by generating the future and devouring the past. This idea inspired Swami Vivekananda's poem, 'Kali, the Mother', which evokes the Night of Kali as a time of pitchy darkness that blots out the stars, while on every side 'a thousand, thousand shades of Death begrimed and black' scatter plagues and sorrows in a mad, joyful dance. In the poet's awesome vision, terror is the goddess's name, death is in her breath, and destruction follows every footfall, for she is the relentless power behind the all-consuming Time.

Ambivalent source of power

Since Kali exists outside society in the wilderness, she does not embrace any societal norms such as caste hierarchy. In the following folk narrative from coastal Andhra Pradesh, Kali bestows a boon on a man who proves his worthiness not by his caste but by his courage.

The low-caste hero Kattavarayan was in love with the high-caste Ariyamalai. He sought permission from his mother, the Devi herself, to abduct her. To test his determination the Devi took the form of Kali in a dark, dense forest. Kattavarayan visited this forest without fear in his heart. He killed all the wild birds and beasts that tried to scare him out. He even killed the demons who guarded the sacred precinct of Kali. Kali hurled numerous weapons at the determined hero, but he managed to dodge each one of them. She finally swallowed him but was forced to spit him out as she could not bear his kicks inside her belly. Convinced of his love for Ariyamalai and his determination to marry her, Kali gave him permission to do as he pleased. To help him in his quest, she gave him a magic drum, a magic sword, various powerful spells and chants, and the knowledge to change his shape at will. But she also warned him, 'Remember, the price of breaking the rules of caste hierarchy is impalement.'

The narrative, however, does not reject caste hierarchy totally. There is clearly a tension between the Kali of the wilderness and the Kali who is worshipped by members of society.

Kali's disregard for social mores led to the belief that she did not care for moral and ethical standards of those who invoked her so long as they satisfied her thirst for blood. This belief made Kali the patron of anarchists, thieves and sorcerers. In the *Bhagavata Purana*, for example, there is a narrative where a band of thieves tries to sacrifice a Brahmin youth to Kali so that their leader gets a son. In the *Adbhuta Ramayana*, the sorcerer Mahi-Ravana tries to sacrifice Rama in order to earn the blessing of Kali. In both these stories, however, the sacrifice never takes place. In the first, the spiritual effulgence of the Brahmin youth scorches the image of Kali, who appears infuriated and kills the thieves. In the other, Rama tricks Mahi-Ravana to place his head on the sacrificial altar and Mahi-Ravana ends up being beheaded by Hanuman. Both these stories thus have a happy ending where the 'bad guys' are destroyed and Kali blesses the 'good guy'. They clearly indicate an attempt to bring Kali within the acceptable social framework. She becomes the upholder of righteousness, the destroyer of villains and demons, who in form looked no different from her erstwhile companions—ghosts and the goblins.

As worship of Kali grew in popularity, there was a conscious effort to restrict the rituals within cultural norms. The Tantrik practice of moving away from cultural norms was shunned by the mainstream society, while the Vedic approach of adapting all rituals to toe the social line became dominant. In the following folktale from Karnataka, Kali is totally domesticated. Like a mother, she finds the pranks of Tenali Raman endearing.

Tenali Raman's father was an impoverished but devoted priest of Kali. One day, he was too ill to go to the temple, so he told his son to go in his place. Raman did not know how to worship the image before him. Since his father had always told him that Kali was his mother, he decided to treat the image as he would his own mother, who had long passed away. He asked her why she did not play with him or feed him or give him a bath as his mother would have. Kali was so touched by this innocent display of devotion that she appeared before him as Dasha-Mukha-Kali, Kali-with-ten-heads. As soon as Tenali Raman saw the ten-headed Kali, he burst into laughter. 'Why are you laughing?' asked Kali, who was used to being saluted when she appeared before devotees. 'Your ten heads make me wonder how you wipe your nose when you have a cold,' replied the lad. The thought made Kali laugh too. Overwhelmed by motherly affection, she offered Tenali Raman a gift: the choice to drink the sweet milk of wealth or the sour curds of intelligence. 'How can I choose without tasting either?' asked

Tenali Raman. Kali let Tenali Raman take a sip of the two drinks. But before she knew it, Tenali Raman finished both the drinks. 'They were both tasty,' said Tenali Raman with a smile on his face. Kali looked at the lad who had outsmarted her in his innocence. Instead of getting upset, she smiled and blessed Tenali Raman, who later became the much-loved court jester of Krishnadevaraya, the ruler of Vijayanagar.

The Worship

The worship of Kali, like the worship of other Hindu deities, involves giving her a form, infusing the form with divinity through appropriate rites and finally adoring the divine entity thus invoked with suitable offerings, including food, flowers, incense, clothes and music. In keeping with the doctrine of devotion, importance is given more to the emotional depth and less to the details of the ritual. The ultimate aim of worshipping Kali in mainstream society is to obtain the blessings of the goddess in matters—both spiritual and material.

Amongst followers of the Tantrik order known as sadhakas, rituals invoking Kali tend to be far more elaborate and complex with the conscious rejection of all things Vedic and the inclusion of objects generally considered inauspicious and activities considered polluting, involving flesh, blood, alcohol, drugs, skulls, funeral ash, dead bodies and sex. Women play an important role in the rituals as they serve as shakti—mediums to realize the goddess. The idea behind these rituals is not to shock a prudish public, but to break through the social conditioning that can be a mental straitjacket to the spiritual aspirant. For a Hindu, the violation of dietary or behavioural taboos, either symbolically or actually, is one way to overturn the neat and tidy preconceptions of social rigidity and be jolted into an altered state of awareness. Only then will the sadhaka achieve the twin goals of attaining spiritual enlightenment and acquiring occult powers.

Before the ritual is undertaken, the sadhaka fulfils all expectations of the guru to prove his worthiness. Then the guru initiates him into the order and prepares him mentally and physically for the arrival of the goddess and the wisdom that will follow. Without this *diksha*, the sadhaka runs the risk of either getting scared by the rites, driven mad by the visions, or coming to the conclusion that the rites are a license for violating rules of civilized conduct.

The instructions vary from scripture to scripture and from guru to guru. The ritual practices tend to be highly individualized to suit the bearings of the sadhaka, but all involve the use of ritual diagrams known as yantras and ritual chants known as mantras.

Tantra

The word 'tantra' refers not only to a school of thought but also to its ritual instructions. Just as the Bhakti school of Hinduism uses emotion, the Gyan school of Hinduism uses intellect and the Karma school uses social conduct to realize the divine, the Tantra school uses ritual practices. Unlike puja, where the emotion accompanying the ritual is greater than the ritual itself, in Tantra the details of the ritual make all the difference.

Below is a set of instructions found in the manuscript

known as *Kali Tantra*. All superlatives have been edited out for the sake of clarity. Please note that Tantrik instructions are unique, depending on the time and place of the ritual and the personalities of the teacher and the student. There is no standard set of instructions. The ones below are from the presiding deity of the manuscript through whom the guru speaks:

Now I speak of the ritual injunction that will help you realize Kali. Doing this, a person becomes like Bhairava. First, I speak of yantra, the knowledge of which conquers death. At first draw a triangle on the sacred altar. Outside, draw another. Then draw three more triangles. Draw a circle and then a beautiful lotus. Then draw another circle and enclose it in a square with four doors. Worship the guru, the six limbs of the body, and the guardians of the directions. Then place your head at the feet of the guru. After worshipping the altar, set down the offering. Place the mantra in the six limbs. Then, in the heart, the ultimate divinity blossoms. Place her at the centre of the yantra by invoking her with your breath. After meditating on the great goddess, dedicate the ritual offerings. Bow to Mahadevi and then worship the surrounding deities. Worship Kali, Kapalini, Kulla,

Kurukulla, Virodhini, Vipracitta in the first two triangles. Then Ugra, Ugraprabha, Dipta in the third triangle. Then Nila, Ghana and Balaka in the outermost triangle. Then Matra, Mudra and Mita within this triangle, and then the very dusky one holding the sword, adorned with human skulls, with her left hand showing the threatening *mudra* and having a pure smile. Worship the eight mothers: Brahmi, Narayani, Maheshvari, Chamunda, Kaumari, Aparajita, Varahi and Narasimhi. In equal shares, give these goddesses animal sacrifice and worship them, smearing them with scent and offering them incense and flame. After doing the puja, worship the Devi using the root mantra. Keep giving food to the Devi time and again. The sadhaka should offer flame ten times. So also offer flowers with the mantra according to the rules of ritual. After meditating on Devi, recite the mantra 1008 times. The fruit of reciting, which is light, place in the hands of the Devi. Then, placing the flower on the head, salute her. With supreme devotion then rub out the yantra.

Yantra

Yantras are geometrical abstractions of divinity that are central to meditation and worship in Tantra. The

Kali Tantra explains how a Kali yantra has to be drawn: 'First, I speak of [Kali] yantra, the knowing of which conquers death. At first draw a triangle. Outside, draw another. Then draw three more triangles. Draw a circle and then a beautiful lotus [with eight petals]. Then draw another circle and then a *bhupura* with four lines and four doors.' Kali's yantra is characterized by five downward pointing triangles superimposed on each other. Each point represents one of the fifteen forms of Kali worshipped on different days of the waning moon. The five triangles are enclosed in a lotus with eight petals. In each petal resides the copulating pair of Bhairava and Bhairavi. This lotus is enclosed in a square bhupura, or enclosure with four gates, leading to the yantra.

A yantra that has not been inscribed with bija mantras (chants) and matrikas (letterings) or that has not been consecrated by an initiated person is unsuitable for worship. To become potent, prana (life) must be installed in a yantra through prescribed rituals, passed on from teacher to student. Every yantra has a definite lifespan, depending on the material. Gold, for example, lasts for life, while silver stays for seven years.

Mantra

A mantra is a potent chant that can be either spoken or written. But it is useless without a yantra or mystical diagram, powerless without diksha or Tantrik initiation and weak without a ritually prescribed tantra or preparatory rite. A mantra has no meaning on its own; its power resides in the sound. One of Kali's popular bija or root mantra is, 'Krim'. The *Kulachudamani Tantra* explains how a mantra may be used:

> On a Tuesday, in the cremation ground, smeared with Kula vermillion, using Kula wood, one should draw a yantra. In the petals write the Chamunda mantra, *'sphrem sphrem kiti kiti'* twice, and then the ninefold mantra of Mahishamardini. Outside this, write the mantras of Jayadurga and Smashana Bhairavi. After writing them, worship Bhadrakali at night, meditating on Kamakhya, the essence of Kamakala.

Image

Krishnanda Agamavagisha wanted to introduce a form of Kali for popular worship in the seventeenth century. The goddess appeared in his dream and advised him to walk towards the south and use the form of the first woman he came upon the next day. Krishnanda did as instructed and came upon a woman who was plastering cow dung cakes on the wall of her house for use as fuel. The woman bit her tongue on seeing Krishnanda, a common habit to express surprise and embarrassment. Her left foot was on a heap of dung, while the other was on the ground. She had raised one hand to plaster the dung cake on the wall, and her other hand was lowered. So it came to pass that the most popular form of Kali depicts her biting her tongue as she steps on Shiva with her left foot, one hand raised to hold the scimitar and the other lowered to hold a severed head.

Many believe this narrative and form is aimed at taming the form of Kali to make it more respectable and suitable for household worship. In Tantrik worship, Kali does not bite her tongue in embarrassment; she stretches it out to drink blood and quench her thirst. Further, Kali does not simply step on Shiva; she copulates with him. While copulating, she is on top, a sexual position known as *viparita rati* or reverse copulation because it is contrary to what is considered acceptable in a patriarchal society where man is always on top of the woman.

So there are two types of images of Kali that are worshipped—the form that is acceptable to the society and the form that is suitable only for those who have renounced society. The former is a respectable, domesticated form of the goddess; the latter is wild and unbridled, accessible only to those who have been adequately initiated and trained in the Tantrik ways.

Place of worship

According to the *Mana-Sara-Shilpa-Shastra*, a treatise on architecture written around the eighth century, temples enshrining the image of Kali must be built far away from villages and towns, near cremation grounds and the dwellings of chandalas, the lowest caste in the Hindu hierarchy, people whose livelihood involves clearing settlements of the dead and watching over funeral pyres. This reinforces Kali's association with the periphery of the Hindu society. In recent times, especially since the nineteenth-century Bengali devotional movement around the idea of Kali, images of Kali are being kept inside the house. But it is often pointed out that the image of Kali located inside homes is different from that which is placed on the border of the village. The former is Dakshina-Kali, the Kali of the 'south' who enlightens, while the latter is Smashana-Kali, the Kali of the 'crematorium' who embraces dirt and pollution.

In most Hindu temples, the image of the deity faces the auspicious east. In many Kali temples, the doorway of the temple may face east but the deity faces the inauspicious west. Kali thus turns her back on conventional, mainstream society, which represses the wild side of Nature for the sake of maintaining social order. In other temples, the image appears as if moving from the south (the direction of mortality) towards the north (the direction of immortality). In the north sits

Kali's consort, Shiva, who is the fountainhead of wisdom and enables man to defy death.

The most popular temple of Kali is located at Kalighat in Kolkata. Other temples of Kali are at Tarapith in Bengal, Kamakhya in Assam and Kathmandu in Nepal.

Time of worship

Tuesday is associated with Mangala or Mars, the celestial body linked with war and death, both of which threaten social stability. It is on this day that Kali is worshipped because she is considered all-powerful then. In many parts of India, this day is dedicated to Ganesha, the son of the Devi, and Hanuman, her servant and protector. Both Ganesha and Hanuman protect devotees from being overwhelmed by the fearsome and wild Kali.

In Hinduism, dawn and the waxing half of the lunar cycle are generally considered auspicious by the Vedic school of thought. The Tantrik school of thought, being counter-culture, prefers midnight and the waning half of the lunar cycle to conduct their rituals. Typically, Kali is worshipped on amavasya or the new moon night at midnight. New moon nights that fall on Tuesdays are especially auspicious.

The most important and elaborate amavasya puja falls in the lunar month corresponding to October or November in the Western calendar. This Night of Kali, more popularly known as Diwali, when most Hindus light lamps while others make blood sacrifices, corresponds with the Samhain, a festival of Celtic druids, a time when according to the Wicca tradition the veil between the material and the spiritual worlds is the thinnest. The choice of this night to worship Kali is appropriate since Kali is, among many things, the goddess of death.

Blood sacrifice

As the form of the Devi that devours life in order to give life, Kali has an insatiable appetite for blood. In Nepal, devotees visiting the Dakshina-Kali temple regularly sacrifice goats, pigs, lambs, buffaloes, and even chickens, pigeons and ducks in order to win favour of the goddess. The heads are chopped or throats slit, and the blood is allowed to flow towards the deity. When a generous amount of blood flows out, men drag the dead animals across the floor of the roofless, outdoor temple to a nearby slaughtering chamber. The shrine's washable, white-tile gutters and floor overflow with sacrificial blood. At Kalighat in Bengal, goats are sacrificed to Kali every Tuesday and during the festival of Diwali.

Two hundred years ago, human sacrifice was common in both these shrines until laws were passed to put an end to the practice, but belief that Kali's favour can be obtained through blood sacrifice remains popular even today. Occasionally, one does hear about a human sacrifice being conducted clandestinely by people who hire the services of criminals to kidnap their victims. More often, people make symbolic sacrifices using vegetables and clay effigies in place of real animals or humans.

The sacrificial beast is always male, never female. The heads that make up Kali's garland, are always those of men. This is because it is through the female form that new life is created and killing one would be tantamount to blocking the cycle of life, something that is unacceptable in Devi worship.

The *Upanishads* declare that the universe is made up of those who eat and that which is eaten. The Devi as the life-giving Gauri or Tripura Sundari or Mangala or Bimala is 'that which is eaten'. The Devi as the life-taking Kali or Tripura Bhairavi or Chamunda or Chandika is 'those who eat'. Thus the Devi embodies the totality of existence.

Lemons, chillies and neem

Those who shy away from blood sacrifice offer Kali sour lemons, pungent chillies and bitter neem. Traditionally, sweet food is considered auspicious and offered to deities. Kali, in her inimical style, rejects all things conventionally considered auspicious and seeks the inauspicious, even in food. Lemons, chillies and neem are a reminder of the vital role played in our lives by those aspects of the cosmos that are generally looked upon with fear, disdain or suspicion.

Alcohol and hallucinogenic drugs

Consumption of alcohol, hallucinogenic drugs such as *Cannabis Indica*, and a variety of mushrooms are condemned in Vedic scriptures as they threaten social stability. These serve as integral components of Kali worship in particular, and Tantrik rites in general. They lead the mind into the subconscious where lie hidden all the suppressed and repressed desires and emotions. One confronts visions unfettered by the shackles of biology and ideology. All that society considers inappropriate and inauspicious is explored and experienced. Thus the divine is realized when truth in its totality is accepted without prejudice.

Corpses

Corpses are considered inauspicious and polluting, hence important in Kali worship. The ritual using corpses is reserved for only highly evolved Tantrik sadhakas who have achieved high levels of consciousness and are hence able to participate in the ritual without a sense of morbid titillation. The ritual usually takes place at midnight of new moon nights falling on Tuesdays. A fresh corpse is chosen, preferably of one who has recently died in battle, or of one who belongs to the caste of warriors, priests or traders. In earlier times, aspirants often waited downstream to collect bodies that were cast into the river. To protect bodies of loved ones, relatives therefore preferred cremating bodies. The corpse is placed face down and his back is used as an altar for invoking Kali. Eating the flesh of corpses is sometimes practised by Aghoras—cremation ground ascetics—who have broken all ties with society and its conventionalities. By treating the corpse as a sacred object, the Tantrik practitioner is forced to re-examine his standards of the auspicious and the inauspicious.

Sexual rites

According to *Brihad Nila Tantra*, the sexual act is an essential component of the ritual aimed at invoking Kali and obtaining powers from her. This is how one scripture describes one aspect of the ritual, while repeatedly clarifying that the ritual is powerful and the information must be kept a secret:

> Have a young and beautiful girl adorned with various jewels. After combing her hair, give her tambula to chew and draw two *Hrims* on her breasts, *Aim* on or near her mouth, and draw two *Klims* on either side of her genitals. Drawing her towards you by her hair, caress

her breasts and then unite. O pure smiling one. Recite the mantra 1000 times, O sweet-faced one. Dearest, one becomes accomplished by practising the rite for a week. Maheshani, recite the mantra not in the manner written in books, but as written in her yoni. This brings mantra siddhi, there is no doubt about it. So, Devi, the secret thing giving all desires has been declared to you. One should not reveal it, one should never reveal it, Maheshani. O Naganandini, at the risk of your life, never reveal it. It is the giver of all siddhi. I cannot speak of the magnificence of this mantra. Had I ten thousand million mouths and ten thousand million tongues, I could still not speak of it, O Paramesvari.

The sexual act is usually illicit—outside marriage, with members of lower castes, and if within the caste, with members of one's own family. Thus all rules and taboos are violated in the quest to obtain Kali's blessing.

The Origin

To understand the rise of Kali as an important member of the Hindu pantheon, one has to appreciate how Hinduism evolved and transformed over 4000 years. In its earliest phase, known as the Vedic period, the focus of Hinduism was on the sacrificial ceremony known as yagna through which priests sought to invoke celestial beings and control the workings of the world. Later, with the rise of heterodox belief systems such as Buddhism in the fifth century BC that challenged ritualism, the Hindu religion became more speculative and monastic. Then, from the fifth century to the fifteenth century AD, Hinduism became increasingly theistic: a personal God came to the fore, shaped in songs and stories, enshrined in temples, invoked and adored through the ritual puja. This process was fuelled by Brahminical appropriation and accommodation of non-Vedic, probably Tantrik, deities, beliefs and practices, which were widespread amongst the masses who, for centuries, had found themselves snubbed by Vedic rituals and intellectual elitism. It is from this non-Vedic space that the goddess now known as Kali in all probability entered the Hindu pantheon along with many other gods and goddesses. But while some deities, like Krishna, Shiva and Durga, could make their way to the centre stage of mainstream Hinduism, Kali always remained at the periphery of Hindu culture—her form challenging even the most accommodating of worshippers.

The name Kali appears for the first time in the *Mundaka Upanishad* written some time around the fifth century BC. There Kali is one of the seven tongues of Agni, the god of fire. But it is not until a thousand years later, after a brief mention in the Mahabharata, that Kali rises to prominence in the *Devi Mahatmya*, also known as the *Chandi Patha*, dated around the sixth century AD. With the compilation of chronicles known as the *Puranas* and the *Tantras* from the fifth to the fifteenth century, Kali's tales were told and her invocations recorded with increasing frequency. The standard iconographic representation, by which Kali is known today in most households, came into being only in the seventeenth century when she became the focus of a popular goddess-based devotional movement in Bengal. Before that, the only representation of Kali was as Chamunda—emaciated, ugly, and dreadful.

Vedic fear and distrust

All Hindus accept that the Vedas form the foundation of Hinduism. These are a set of scriptures that include compilations of hymns known as the *Samhitas*, ritual manuals known as *Brahmanas*, ascetic speculations known as *Aranyakas*, and metaphysical discourses known as the *Upanishads*. These were compiled between 2000 BC and 500 BC by cattle-herding Indo-European tribes called Aryans, who came to dominate the Indian subcontinent around this time.

There is no mention of Kali in the *Rig Samhita*, which reached its final form around 1500 BC. The focus is on male deities such as Indra, Agni and Soma. Female goddesses are mentioned infrequently and generally play a minor role. Most Vedic goddesses such as the dawn-goddess Usha, the earth-goddess Prithvi, the speech-goddess Vach, and the mother-goddess Aditi, are benign. But there is one called Nirriti (meaning 'decay') who is associated with destruction and death. Hymns request this goddess to stay away. She is described as having dark complexion, wearing dark clothes and residing in the south. Many scholars are of the opinion that Nirriti is the Vedic Kali.

The *Jaiminya Brahmana* dated around the eighth century BC tells the story of Dirgha-jihvi, an ogress, who like Kali has a long tongue and insatiable sexual appetite.

Dirgha-jihvi or 'the long-tongued one' used to lick up the divine drink, Soma—produced during the yagna—that was much loved by the gods. Exasperated by her actions, Indra, king of the gods, wanted to grab her, but he could not get hold of her. So he said, 'Let no one perform any sacrifices at all, for Dirgha-jihvi licks up the Soma produced.' Now, Sumitra, the son of Kutsa, was handsome. Indra said to him, 'Go seduce Dirgha-jihvi.' When Sumitra approached her, she said, 'You have just one sexual organ, but I have many, one on each limb. This won't work.' Sumitra went back and informed Indra of his failure. 'I will create sexual organs for you on every limb,' said Indra. Equipped with these, Sumitra went back to her. This time she welcomed him with open arms. They lay together. As soon as he had his way with her, he remained firmly stuck in her. Finding the ogress pinned to the ground, Indra struck her down with his thunderbolt.

The fear of Nirriti and the demonization of Dirgha-jihvi have led to speculations that these hymns express the discomfort of the patriarchal Aryans each time they encountered the Kali-like goddesses worshipped by the non-Aryan agricultural communities, who were probably matriarchal.

A century or two after the *Jaiminya Brahmana*, the Vedic priests put together the *Mundaka Upanishad*, where Kali is the name of one of the seven quivering tongues of the fire-god Agni, whose flames devour sacrificial oblations and transmit them to the gods. The verse characterizes Agni's seven tongues as black, terrifying, swift as thought, intensely red, smoky coloured, sparkling and radiant. Significantly, the first two adjectives, kali ('black') and karali ('terrifying'), recur in later texts to describe the horrific aspect of the goddess. Karali additionally means 'having a gaping mouth and protruding teeth'.

Between the third century BC and third century AD, one finds clearer evidence of appropriation of non-Vedic deities, beliefs and practices. Kali first appears unequivocally as a goddess in the *Kathaka Grihyasutra*, a ritualistic text that names her in a list of Vedic deities to be invoked with offerings of perfume during the marriage ceremony. Unfortunately, the text reveals nothing more about her. In the Mahabharata and Ramayana that were being composed around this time, goddesses, including Kali, are given more character; they are usually independent and (hence) wild, appearing as manifestations of divine rage and embodiments of the forces of destruction. In the Mahabharata, for example, the nocturnal bloodbath by Ashwatthama at the end of the eighteen-day war, when the innocent children of the Pandavas are slaughtered rather dastardly while they are asleep, is seen as the work of 'Kali of bloody mouth and eyes, smeared with blood and adorned with garlands, her garment reddened—holding noose in hand—binding men and horses and elephants with her terrible snares of death'.

Non-Vedic and pre-Aryan

Despite the importance given to the Vedas in modern Hinduism, it is clear to scholars that Hindu practices such as plant-, animal-, mineral- and idol-worship have roots in non-Vedic, probably pre-Aryan, times. Unfortunately, until the script of the Indus valley civilization is deciphered or some other epigraphic discovery is made, there will be no evidence, only speculation about the extent and nature of this pre-Vedic milieu that let itself be dominated by the Vedic ideology without losing its hold in the spiritual imagination of the common man.

Study of the early history of India is a highly contentious field. Much of the past is irretrievably lost, and attempts to assemble the surviving fragments are all too often coloured by feelings of nationalism, ethnic pride, religious belief, lingering resentment towards colonialism, and the legacy of the pioneering European scholars who injected their own Judeo-Christian prejudices and view of history into an area where they clearly do not belong. Today, wildly conflicting theories abound, and even the best are not without serious anomalies. Therefore at present there is simply no way to make sense of all the data at hand. Nevertheless, it is safe to say that Indian religion, throughout its long history, has always consisted of two intertwining strands—the Vedic and the Tantrik—with the latter including everything that is not Vedic.

For many, the great Indus valley civilization stretching from the western shores of the Indus river to the eastern shores of the Ganga was the heartland of Tantrik ideology, rooted in goddess-worship, fertility, magic and shamanism. This urban civilization was at its peak around 2500 BC and waned in significance around 1500 BC, about the same time that the Vedic ideology came to dominate the land. This has led many scholars to reach the highly contentious conclusion that the Aryans probably overran and perhaps assimilated the Indus valley civilization.

Recent research suggests that climatic changes, rather than invasions or unchecked immigrations, were responsible for the collapse of the Indus valley civilization. Since hymns in the Vedas refer to a mighty river Saraswati that dried up, forcing the Aryans to move east towards the Ganga, many scholars have come to believe that the Indus valley civilization was in all probability the Saraswati civilization. They hypothesize that like most urban centres, the cities of the Indus–Saraswati valleys accommodated various belief systems from the patriarchal Vedas to the matriarchal Tantra. They point to the city at Kalibangan where archaeologists discovered what appears to be a series of seven Vedic fire altars, while years of excavation at the same site has yielded two goddess figurines. In contrast, the contemporaneous cities of Mohenjodaro and Harappa were centres of thriving goddess cults, attested by the recovery of thousands of figurines of goddess from the ruins.

Archaeological sites in Zhob and Kulli valleys, in the hills of Baluchistan, have revealed peasant cultures that predate the Indus valley civilization. These isolated hamlets produced female figurines of baked clay. Most interpreters believe that these idols had a ritual purpose and were in all probability fertility goddesses. That the features of these figurines border on the grotesque has led many to conclude that these goddesses were intended to inspire horror and may have served as a prototype for later-day images of fearsome goddesses like Kali.

The *Matsya Purana* suggests that Kali originated as a tribal goddess indigenous to one of India's inaccessible mountainous regions, Mount Kalanjara in north central India, east of the Indus valley floodplain. But owing to the date of the *Purana's* composition, this evidence regarding Kali's place of origin cannot be taken as particularly reliable.

The earliest documentary evidence of worship of wild and independent goddesses outside the Vedic fold comes from Tamil Sangam literature dated from third century BC to third century AD. It mentions the Kali-like goddess of war and victory, Korravai, to whom buffaloes were sacrificed and for whom forest warriors, the Marvars, were exhorted to ritual suicide.

Tantrik roots

It is not clear whether Tantrik practices were a reactionary rejection of Vedic values, or whether Vedic taboos evolved only to stay away from Tantrik pollution. But for as long as Tantrik and Vedic religions have coexisted on Indian soil, they have influenced each other. The earliest Vedic hymns, dated 2000 BC, are tinged with Tantrik elements, and at the heart of Tantra scriptures, dated no earlier than AD 600, lies the sublime metaphysical philosophy of the *Upanishads*, which form the culmination of Vedic thought. Be that as it may, there are clear distinguishing features between the two tributaries of Hindu thought. Tantra views the world not as maya or delusion, as Vedic metaphysicians claim, but as the source of power, shakti. In the Tantrik scheme of things, it is not caste or gender that determines one's accessibility of spiritual wisdom as in the Vedic world, but one's worthiness in the eyes of the guru. Female forms embody enchantment and temptation in Vedic mythology, but in Tantrik narratives they take the form of powerful wilful deities who are privy to the mysteries of life and who need to be appeased or forced into revealing their secrets. This is the cultural matrix from which Kali emerged—a world of fertility, magic, sacrifice, the deification of natural forces, mind–body control, and lofty speculation over the nature of reality.

Cults of Kali or her manifestations are in evidence

from amongst the earliest Tantrik texts. Her worship was popular among cremation-ground ascetics such as the Aghoras and wandering alchemist–sorcerers of the Nav Nath tradition, who invoked Kali and practised yoga in order to acquire eight siddhis or occult powers that would enable them to change shape or size, defy the laws of space and time, and perform miraculous feats.

In the *Jayadrathayamala*, Kali is identified with states of consciousness. The *Nigama-kalpataru* and the *Picchila Tantra* declare that of all mantras Kali's is the greatest. The *Yogini Tantra*, the *Kamakhya Tantra* and the *Niruttara Tantra*, all proclaim Kali the greatest of all forms of the Devi. In the *Nirvana Tantra*, the gods Brahma, Vishnu and Shiva are said to arise from her like bubbles from the sea, endlessly arising and passing away, leaving their source unchanged. The *Kamada Tantra* states unequivocally that Kali is attributeless, neither male nor female, pure, and the imperishable supreme reality known in the *Upanishads* as the Brahman from which the universe manifests and into which it returns.

Rituals to invoke Kali, documented as in the *Kulachudamani Tantra*, *Karpuradistotra* and *Niruttara Tantra*, involved flesh, blood, funeral ash, skulls, alcohol, hallucinogens, corpses, sex—everything that was considered inauspicious and polluting by the Brahminical order. These rituals were a closely guarded secret, restricted to those initiated into the Tantrik order. For the rest, Kali seemed like a distant goddess who was far removed from conventional social values and who was willing to bestow power on anyone, even those with questionable moral and ethical standards, who satisfied her craving for blood. This fear and suspicion of Kali expressed itself in popular literature and secular texts of the medieval period, which have been less than sympathetic to the goddess, often painting a lurid and truly horrifying picture of Kali, exacting and demanding human sacrifice. For instance, in Bhavabhuti's play *Malati Madhava*, written in the eighth century, the heroine is abducted by a witch who seeks to sacrifice her at the altar of Chamunda in order to acquire occult powers.

Rise of theism

Following the rise and fall of Buddhism in India, Hinduism went through a radical change. The old Vedic order collapsed and a new form of spirituality came to dominate the land, one that involved the adoration of a personal god. Three deities vied for supremacy in the new order: Shiva, Vishnu and Mahadevi. Their followers were known as Shaivas, Vaishnavas and Shaktas respectively. Their narratives and rituals were recorded in chronicles known as the *Puranas*. One such *Purana*, the *Markandeya*, contains within it the foundational text of all subsequent Hindu Devi cults. This book within a book is known as the *Devimahatmya*, the *Shri Durga Saptashati*, or the *Chandi Patha*, which describes the triumph of the Devi as Durga over demons such as Mahisha, Madhu and Kaitabha, and Shumbha and Nishumbha.

The seventh chapter of *Devimahatmya* describes Kali springing forth from the furrowed brow of the goddess Durga in order to slay the demons Chanda and Munda, generals of Shumbha and Nishumbha. Here, Kali's horrific form has black, loosely hanging, emaciated flesh that barely conceals her angular bones. Gleaming white fangs protrude from her gaping, bloodstained mouth, framing her lolling red tongue. Sunken, reddened eyes peer out from her black face. She is clad in a tiger's skin and carries a khatvanga, a skull-topped staff traditionally associated with tribal shamans and magicians, one that suggests Kali's origin amongst fierce, aboriginal people. In the ensuing battle, much attention is placed on her gaping mouth and gnashing teeth, which devour the demon hordes. At one point, Munda hurls thousands of discuses at her, but they enter her mouth 'as so many solar orbs vanishing into the denseness of a cloud'. The eighth chapter of the *Devimahatmya* paints an even more gruesome portrait. Having slain Chanda and Munda, Kali is now called

Chamunda, and she faces an infinitely more powerful adversary in the demon named Rakta-bija. Whenever a drop of his blood falls on earth, an identical demon springs up. When utter terror seizes the gods, Durga merely laughs and instructs Kali to drink the drops of blood. While Durga assaults Rakta-bija so that his blood runs copiously, Kali avidly laps it up. The demons who spring into being from the flow perish between her gnashing teeth until Rakta-bija topples drained and lifeless to the ground.

Subsequent *Puranas* such as the *Shiva, Linga, Vamana, Matsya, Bhagavat,* and the *Devi Bhagavata* contain narratives through which Kali's position within the orthodox fold in relation to other deities, both male and female, was clearly established. In most places, she was seen as a wild form of Uma-Parvati—the consort of Shiva, and the mother of Ganesha and Kartikeya—who needed to be tamed for the sake of cosmic stability.

Interestingly, in Bengal where mainstream devotional movements inspired by Chaitanya often crossed paths with popular Tantrik beliefs and customs, Kali came to be identified with another dark god, the cowherd Krishna, perhaps in a spirit of syncretism. This trend reaches its peak in the *Tantraraja Tantra,* where it is said that having already charmed the world of men, the Devi took a male form as Krishna and then proceeded to enchant women. The *Kalivilasa Tantra,* a Bengali work, states that Krishna was born as the son of the golden Gauri and turned black when he was excited by passion. In the *Todala Tantra*, each of the ten Maha-Vidyas, forms of the supreme Devi, has her own male counterpart and here Krishna is said to be the spouse of Kali.

Despite this, Kali continued to be treated with ambivalence by orthodox Brahminical traditions, owing to her association with cremation grounds, untouchable castes and tribals, and her fondness for flesh, blood and alcohol.

Into the mainstream

Kali worship in mainstream religion had less to do with her mention in Tantrik texts or Puranic scriptures, and more to do with her identification with village-goddess cults such as Bhagavati of Kerala, Yellamma of Karnataka, Kalu Bai of Maharashtra, Tara of Bengal, Bhadra-Kali of Andhra, Kalika Mata of Gujarat and Rajasthan, and Mari Amman of Tamil Nadu. She is the fierce guardian of the frontiers, the dark side of grama-devi who threatens disease and disaster unless appeased with blood-sacrifices, self-mutilation, hook-swinging, fire-walking and offerings of bridal finery.

As Kali moved from esoteric Tantrik rites into household shrines, the idea of a goddess who disregards conventional ethics and morality became unpalatable.

There was a conscious effort to make her culturally more sensitive and ethically more responsible. Thus in the following narrative from *Adbhuta Ramayana* the tables are turned, with Kali's blessings, on the sorcerer who tries to sacrifice Rama.

Rama raised an army of monkeys and launched an attack on the island-kingdom of Lanka to rescue his wife Sita who had been abducted by the demon-king Ravana. Fearing Rama would be successful in his mission, Ravana sought the help of his son Mahi-Ravana, a sorcerer. Mahi-Ravana abducted Rama and took him to his subterranean kingdom, intent on sacrificing him to the goddess Kali. Rama's monkey-lieutenant, Hanuman, followed Mahi-Ravana to the temple of Kali, where he learnt from the goddess that she did not desire the blood of Rama. With her help, Hanuman devised a plan to outwit Mahi-Ravana. When it was time for the sacrifice, Rama refused to place his head on the altar, as advised by Hanuman. 'I am a prince. I have never bowed my head. Show me how,' said Rama. Mahi-Ravana was forced to demonstrate. He lowered his head on the altar. No sooner had Mahi-Ravana's neck touched the altar than Hanuman rushed forward and beheaded the sorcerer. Kali drank the sorcerer's blood and blessed Rama and Hanuman. Since that day, Hanuman has become the guardian of Kali temples.

In the seventeenth century, Kali's characterization underwent a radical change in Bengal. Rather than being visualized as an emaciated bloodthirsty crone, she came to be seen as a voluptuous beauty. Lofty spiritual meanings were propped up wherever her image was unsettling. This loss of fierceness had its roots in a devotional movement popularized by the Tantrik Krishnanda Agamavagisha, who in his *Tantrasara* described for the first time, amongst other things, what is now the standard form of Dakshina-Kali.

Devotees began visualizing Kali as a 'loving caring mother', thanks to the songs of the mystic Ramprasad Sen (1718–75) who had visions of her. Legend has it that Ramprasad had obtained a job as a bookkeeper with an accountant. However, he wrote Tara—the name by which he addressed Kali—all over in the ledgers. The employer saw this and recognized a saint in the making. Ramprasad used to wade into the river Ganga and sing the songs in honour of the divine mother. Boats sailing down the Ganga would stop to listen to his songs, people dying on the banks of the river would ask Ramprasad to sing to them. He soon became the favourite of the king. His songs had a profound impact on local culture. The nineteenth-century saint Ramakrishna, guru of Swami Vivekananda, often quoted the songs during his discourses.

O Mother! You have great dissolution in your
hand;
Shiva lies at your feet, absorbed in bliss.
You laugh aloud, striking terror
Streams of blood flow from your limbs.
O Tara, doer of good, the good of all, giver of
safety,
O Mother, grant me safety.
O Mother Kali! Take me in your arms
O Mother Kali! Take me in your arms
O Mother! Come now as Tara with a smiling
face and clad in white;
As dawn descends on dense darkness of the
night.
O Mother! Terrific Kali! I have worshipped you
alone so long.
My worship is finished; now O Mother, bring
down your sword.

It was through the images and songs of this Bengali devotional movement and the influence it had on Bengali scholars who interacted with the West, such as Swami

Vivekananda and Shri Aurobindo, that Kali became known across the world. A great contribution to the understanding of Kali was also made by Sir John Woodroffe (1865–1936), who, while serving as a High Court judge in Kolkata during the British Raj, found time to translate little-known Tantrik texts and comment on them without the typical European condescension under the pseudonym Arthur Avalon.

The Metamorphosis

The Metamorphosis

Kali's unconventional form has made her the central figure in many strategic political discourses. The most popular of these was the nineteenth-century propaganda of the British East India Company that made her the patron of highway robbers known as Thugs. Around the same time, Bengali intellectuals, tired of apologizing and defending Hindu practices including the macabre rites associated with Tantra and linked to Kali, transformed the goddess into Bharat Mata, a powerful symbol of the oppressed motherland who sought liberation from the foreign yoke. In the twentieth century, Kali's rejection of patriarchal values made her a powerful symbol within the feminist movement. She also caught the attention of New Age writers seeking to shed the Judeo-Christian-Islamic legacy of the West, and reclaim Devi worship. Kali's ambivalence has inspired the creative mind and led to her incorporation in many works of fiction, though not always in a flattering light.

Devi of Thugs

Between the cities of Allahabad and Benaras, where the Vindhya mountain range touches the southern bank of the holy Ganga, in a town known as Vindhyachal stands the temple complex devoted to the goddess Vindyavasini, a form of Durga. Not far from this shrine is the temple of Kalikhoh, believed to be the central shrine of the Thugs who became infamous thanks to the writings of many officers of the British East India Company.

The officers wrote that Thugs lived outwardly respectable lives, usually as craftsmen. But for a few weeks each year they dedicated themselves to the slaughter that was their act of worship. Operating far from home to avoid being recognized, gangs of ten to fifty Thugs lured victims to their death through deception. They joined traders and pilgrims and accompanied them until a chance for murder arose. When the time was right, the assassins approached victims from behind, and strangled them with rumals or handkerchiefs, all the while whispering to Kali to watch. The following story was told to explain this bizarre practice:

> When Kali was confronted by the demon Rakta-bija who could reproduce clones of himself from every drop of his blood, she created out of her sweat two fierce warriors—Kala Bhairav and Gora Bhairav. Kali gave them two rumals with instructions to strangulate the Rakta-bija clones so that no blood was spilt on the ground. The Thugs were descendants of the two Bhairavs, who strangulated their victims to demonstrate their devotion to the family deity.

Some travellers were spared the attack. Women, for

instance, were usually spared in deference to Kali's gender. So were hermits and craftsmen. Lepers and cripples were exempt, since the thugs feared contamination. Not wanting to risk reprisal from colonial rulers, the killers never molested Europeans either. Most preferred victims were men from the upper castes—either Brahmins, or baniyas (traders), or Rajputs (warriors).

In 1826, Colonel William Sleeman, the civil administrator of the Jubbulpore (Jabalpur) district in Central India, set about suppressing the Thugs. He turned to captured Thugs to augment his information about the secret brotherhood, breaking their code of silence with offers of clemency. Entire gangs were rounded up and subjected to harsh punishment. By 1840, over 3500 Thugs were tried and 500 were hanged. By 1858, except for isolated outbreaks, the reign of Thug terror came to an end. (Some of the reformed Thugs became skilled carpet weavers, so skilled that one of their carpets was commissioned by Queen Victoria for Windsor Castle.)

Although the tale of this bizarre cult of thieves has since captured the imagination of the people across the world, inspiring many novels and films, recent research by scholars such as Stewart N. Gordon has convincingly shown that the Thugs were neither a religious order nor any kind of organized, homogeneous group. Those labelled as Thugs were in fact teams of marauding soldiers—both Hindu and Muslim—from various regions who stole and killed not out of religious compulsion but from economic and political motives. They were ordered by their leaders to extort cash needed for purchasing weapons and paying mercenaries who would fight with the British. Many of these soldiers worshipped Kali, not because she 'gave power to those who quenched her thirst for blood', but merely because she was the traditional patron of martial orders in the region. Since their activities hurt the economic and political ambitions of the British East India Company, they were strategically, systematically, and successfully stigmatized through propaganda writings that took advantage of the ambivalent feelings of the masses towards Kali. The British then proceeded to wipe out these bands of thieves in the 1830s. During this period, anyone associated with the Vindhyachal temples, especially Kalikhoh, became suspect, particularly if he belonged to a warrior caste. As a result, the temple of Kali turned into a dilapidated condition. Even today, locals take great pains to dissociate the shrine from Thugs and their 'bizarre' rites. So much so that people deny the Tantrik roots of both Kali and Vindhyavasini, and prefer to view her as a milder, Vedic, vegetarian goddess.

Demon mother

While the tale of the thugs and their association with Kali may have been a strategic narrative of British colonialists to generate popular opinion against their political enemies, it was based on popular beliefs about Kali that associate her with thieves (as we find in the story of Bharata in the *Bhagavata Purana*) and sorcerers (in the story of Mahi-Ravana in the *Adbhuta Ramayana*). Such has been the success of the Thug narrative that it has, since the nineteenth century, inspired many novels and films where Kali plays a central role. In the Jules Verne classic *Around the World in Eighty Days*, we learn:

> The travellers crossed, beyond Malligaum, the fatal country so often stained with blood by the sectaries of the goddess Kali . . . It was thereabouts that Feringhea, the Thuggee chief, king of the stranglers, held his sway. These ruffians, united by a secret bond, strangled victims of every age in honour of the goddess Death, without ever shedding blood; there was a period when this part of the country could scarcely be travelled over without corpses being found in every direction. The English Government has succeeded in greatly diminishing these murders, though the Thuggees still exist,

and pursue the exercise of their horrible rites . . .
All this portion of Bundelcund, which is little
frequented by travellers, is inhabited by a
fanatical population, hardened in the most
horrible practices of the Hindoo faith.

In the film *Indiana Jones and the Temple of Doom*,
second of the Indiana Jones trilogy, created by Steven
Spielberg and George Lucas, the villain is one Mola Ram,
chief of the Thugs, enslaver of children, the 'shaman'
who sacrifices humans to satisfy Kali's thirst for blood
and obtain magical powers from her. Such unflattering
portrayal of Kali is also seen in the American television
series 'The Far Pavilion', where Kali is the patron deity
of the villainous old king and is described as the 'black
goddess of death and drinker of blood'. In the British
television series 'The Jewel in the Crown', when an
Englishwoman expresses her desire to see a 'Hindoo'
temple, the only temple the director wishes to show, of
all the gods and goddesses in the Hindu pantheon, is
the one of Kali.

While the description of Kali in these novels and
films is not incorrect, the focus is clearly on the dark
and demonic sides of the goddess, one that has the ability
to shock readers/viewers and satisfy their search for the
exotic in India. The resulting fallout has been that Kali,
with her fondness for sacrifice and links with the occult,

has become in the eyes of many the Hindu counterpart of the Devil. This is ironic and unfortunate, as Hinduism does not endorse the concept of evil so critical in Judeo-Christian-Islamic thought. There is no Devil in Hindu mythology either. In the Hindu worldview, things may be socially inappropriate, but everything is a manifestation of the divine. Negative events are explained not as the work of the Devil but as results of bad karma. Fierce deities, such as Kali, with their macabre rites are never seen as demons—only as the darker aspects of divinity. To the Western eye, informed by the Biblical discourse, such ideas made little sense. The only way an image of a naked female deity who demands blood sacrifice can make sense is by viewing her as loathsome, terrible, malignant—the Indian counterpart of the Biblical Lilith, the Devil's concubine and the mother of demons.

When Indian filmmakers produce horror films based on Hollywood scripts they often find it difficult to identify a local counterpart of the Devil and end up force-fitting Kali in the role. The problems with this approach are obvious. In the intial part of the film, Kali is represented as the patron of the villain, giving him magical powers when he offers her the blood of innocents. In the final act of the film, after hearing the hero's passionate appeal, she turns against the villain and becomes the divine deliverer. The ambivalence towards Kali is evident in Bollywood films such as *Karan Arjun* and teleserials like 'Kya Haadsa, Kya Hakikat'. Kali remains the favourite of filmmakers trying to scare their audience. Thus in *Sangharsh*, a film based on the *Silence of the Lambs*, the serial killer is a deranged male-to-female transvestite who believes that he will attain immortality by sacrificing young children to—who else but Kali.

Bharat Mata

The arrival of Western education systems in India in the nineteenth century forced Indians to accept the backward nature of many traditional beliefs and customs such as child marriage and caste system. Exposed to Western ideology and Christianity, many intellectuals were embarrassed by many things Hindu, including worship of plants, animals and idols. This led to Hindu Renaissance in the nineteenth century, during which a concerted effort was made to reform Indian society and cleanse Hinduism of outdated practices.

An offshoot of this cultural movement was the belief in Indian nationhood. The belief expressed itself through the idea of Bharat Mata, the goddess who embodied the Indian nation. She was the mother of all Indians and it was the duty of all Indians to protect her honour without regard for personal hardship and sacrifice.

Bankim Chandra Chatterjee's novel *Anandamath*

played a critical role in the popularity of this idea. In the novel, the hero Mahendra finds that the image of the unfamiliar goddess Bharat Mata is no different from that of the familiar Kali. He is informed that Kali's dark, gaunt, dishevelled and naked figure indicates a nation that has been reduced to poverty, nakedness and chaos by foreign rulers. The severed arms that adorn Kali's waist as a girdle are the arms of devotees who will have to be sacrificed before the mother can be freed from her foreign yoke.

Bankim Chandra Chatterjee's Kali is not the object of worship. Her form has no mystical significance. She is simply a symbol of the condition of India under the British rule: a place of sickness, death, poverty and exploitation. This interpretation of Kali's nakedness reveals the discomfort of the nineteenth-century Indian intellectual with the form of Kali. He could not explain her nakedness, her unabashed sexuality, her bloodlust, her association with thieves and sorcerers either to himself or to the British rulers of the land, or to missionaries who were eager to associate Kali-worship with primitive superstition, witchcraft and Satanic rites. By giving her form a political interpretation, the Indian intellectual found himself no longer on the backfoot. In fact, it gave him the springboard to challenge the then-existing political condition.

Goddess in feminism

The idea of a goddess who steps on a male deity and does not assume a form that is pleasing to the male eye has great appeal to feminists, both in India and in the West. This has led to Kali becoming the patron goddess of many feminists in the twentieth century.

Kali has helped many feminist writers by serving as the perfect symbol that affirms the female body, female sexuality, female anger and female aggression, which have been silenced or denied for centuries by male-dominated society, apparently to ensure social stability. Overshadowed for centuries by more desirable and benevolent forms of the Devi such as Lakshmi and Gauri, Kali has been found to be more compatible with the reality of a plundered earth and wounded womanhood, poised to strike back and assert itself. Feminists believe that the reality of Kali is so frightening that male narrators and artists have consciously chosen to either sideline or demonize her over the centuries.

During the freedom struggle, while men saw the Devi as Bharat Mata, a warrior goddess calling them to take up arms on behalf of the country, women began visualizing her as Kali who egged them on to defy patriarchal norms and stand up for their rights. Scholars such as Sumanta Banerjee have uncovered folk songs from eighteenth-century Bengal, sung by women belonging to lower rungs in the socio-economic order, where the defiance and protest is expressed through the imagery of Kali standing on top of her husband, Shiva.

> The hussy has thrown the bloke flat on his back,
> With her foot on his chest.
> Wordless she stands, glaring in anger.

Research by Sanjukta Gupta has revealed that even in medieval India, women saints such as Akka-Mahadevi of Karnataka, Karaikal Ammaiyar of the Tamils, and Lalla-Ded of Kashmir expressed their social and spiritual autonomy by abandoning their clothes, ornaments and cosmetics, and by leaving their hair dishevelled and unbound, perhaps emulating Kali, the undomesticated form of the Devi.

Reclaiming the goddess

A study of Hindu scriptures suggests that the form today described as Kali was viewed as a demoness in the Vedic era and that with the passage of time, with the increasing vocalization of folk traditions within the classical Brahminical framework and the rising respectability of Tantrik ideology, she became progressively identified with divinity, ultimately becoming one of the most-favoured manifestations of the Devi.

However, many scholars, especially feminist writers from the West, reject this view. They believe that the first form of the divine visualized by humans, even before the first scriptures were written, was female. This visualization took place when human civilization was at its infancy, in the hunter–gatherer stage, before there were cities or settled communities. The female form of the divine symbolized humankind's awe at Nature's ability to give and take life. With the passage of time, it was clear that to harness Nature's resources, domestication of Nature was essential. The goddess had to be tamed. And to justify her domestication and suppression, she had to be demonized. The deities who tamed wild nature became the new gods—they were all male. With this, human society became patriarchal. And it was in the patriarchal phase of human civilization that the first books such as the *Rig Samhita* came into being, where female deities were either sidelined or demonized.

This feminist insight into the evolution of religions is based on the fact that in most major religions today the form taken by God (whether Yahweh or Bhagavan), prophet (whether Moses or Muhammad), or saviour (whether Jesus or the Boddhisattva) is male, although Stone- and Bronze-Age archaeological sites tend to reveal more images of female deities.

Scholars such as Barbara G. Walker believe that the Devi-based religion practised in prehistoric times was quite homogeneous. She claims that Indo-European linguistic roots account for many similar names and figures spread over large geographical areas. In her estimation, Finland's Kalma and Ireland's Cailleach derive from the same Sanskrit root as Kali.

In the book *Dancing in the Flames*, Marion Woodman and Elinor Dickson look at Kali through the lens of Jungian psychology and see her primarily as a transformer. They conclude that true transformation lies in the death of the ego and in releasing all the false values that the ego clings to out of fear.

The feminist hypothesis has led to an urgent need in parts of the world to reclaim Devi-worship within current theological systems and to revive Devi-worship, long forgotten. In a setting that respects all religions and draws on the practices of several, Kali remains overwhelmingly authentic, with certain facets of her personality merely emphasized or de-emphasized to suit the radically different circumstances of her new followers and surroundings. She is both the maternal goddess praised by Ramprasad Sen and the fierce devourer of the *Devi Mahatmya*. Her unconditional love promises her devotees dignity and acceptance, regardless of sexual orientation, race, and economic or social standing.

The Wisdom

There are three approaches to understanding the mystery that is Kali. One is the path of the vira or the hero adopted by the Tantrik initiate. Then there is the path of the bhakta or the devotee adopted by the householder. Finally, there is the path of the gyani or the sage adopted by metaphysicians and intellectuals.

Path of the hero

According to Tantra, a hero is one who is willing to boldly face the darkest aspects of reality, embodied in the goddess Kali. The hero's mystical journey or sadhana begins after he proves his worthiness by fulfilling all the conditions laid down by the guru. He is then initiated into the Tantrik fold. Following the initiation ceremony known as diksha, the guru systematically challenges the student to face his fears and question his views on morality and purity. He is asked to eat what he has never dared to eat, look at things he has never dared to see, hear things he has never dared to hear, and do things he has never dared to do. If he is a vegetarian, he is made to eat meat. If he is a non-vegetarian, he is asked to eat beef. If he has eaten beef, he is asked to eat human flesh. If he has eaten human flesh, he is asked to eat rotting meat. The hero is asked to drink alcohol and consume hallucinogenic drugs that force him to reveal his innermost secrets and face his secret desires. He is asked to have illicit sex. All the while his guide is his guru and his deity is Kali.

The guru helps the student cultivate an aggressive, fearless stance before Kali. The hero challenges Kali to unveil her most forbidding secrets. The hero seeks to appropriate the truths embodied in Kali by confronting her boldly. These truths, that life feeds on death, that death is inevitable, that time wears things, that sex is the most primal and creative instinct of all living creatures, are fearsome if denied or repressed. Those in denial of life's primal truths are afraid of Kali. The hero who accepts these truths confronts Kali without fear.

This heroic approach is evident in a folk narrative of Andhra Pradesh:

> She stood as tall as the palm tree. She projected twelve spears from her head and impaled an elephant on each spear. On the elephants she stacked twelve corpses. She had twelve lamps on each corpse. She held weapons in all her twelve hands. With jingling bells on her feet and burning coals on her head she came taking huge strides. She yelled like thunder. Fire rose from the sky and sparks of fire fell on the earth. Biting her teeth fiercely she puffed her mouth and blew whirlwinds. Ghosts followed her and let out shrill cries. The hero, Katamaraju, stood his ground defiantly, unafraid, winning her admiration and affection.

Path of the devotee

The approach of the devotee to Kali is quite different in mood and temperament from the approach of the hero. The devotee approaches Kali as a helpless child goes to his mother. She may be terrible, even hostile, yet he has no choice but to turn to her for security, warmth and support. This devotional approach shaped itself in eighteenth-century Bengal where Ramprasad Sen, one of the leaders of this movement, declared, 'Just as a child clings to his mother even when beaten by her, the devotees of Kali must surrender themselves to Kali despite her ferocious appearance.'

Kali, as the object of devotion and adoration, continues to be the bloodthirsty, naked goddess who wanders in crematoriums. She is anything but motherly. Unlike goddesses such as Mangala-Gauri, Bimala and Lalita, she is neither beautiful nor fertile. She does not give life; she takes life. She does not nourish or nurture; she tortures and kills. She is neither docile nor gentle; her sexuality is unbridled, her violence untamed.

When the devotee calls Kali 'Mother', he adopts the attitude of a child, whose essential nature towards its mother is that of acceptance, no matter how awful, how indifferent, how fearsome she is. The devotee, then, by making the apparently unlikely assertion that Kali is his mother, enables himself to approach and appropriate the forbidding truths that Kali reveals. In appropriating these truths, the devotee, like the hero, is liberated from the fear these truths impose on people who deny or ignore them.

Through devotion, the devotee no longer fears death, decay or ugliness. He is not disappointed in terms of worldly desires and pleasures. He accepts things as they are. He is reconciled to the reality that is life. He realizes that judgements are based on standards and that standards are artificial. Free from all standards, liberated by wisdom, he embraces Kali and enjoys her game.

Path of the sage

While the devotee approaches Kali emotionally, the sage approaches her intellectually. He tries to understand why she appears the way she does. What is the meaning behind her horrific appearance? The initial revulsion is questioned, the fear introspected. He finds that in her form and her worship there is a conscious effort to embrace all that conventional society distances itself from: unbridled sex and violence, lack of control, and celebration of ugliness and decay. Kali reverses all cultural standards—bad things become good in her worship, the inauspicious becomes auspicious. Death and blood, which are considered polluting, become Kali's adornments. Meat and alcohol that 'good' people stay away from, are central to her worship. Decent women may cover their bodies, bind their hair, deny their sexuality and live lives of self-denial and self-discipline, but Kali dances naked with hair unbound, unaffected by the disapproving stares of those around. By behaving thus, Kali forces the individual to look at all things one fears, represses, denies and suppresses, things that exist outside man-made moral and ethical codes, things that fill life with uncertainty and restlessness.

The sage realizes that culture is an artificial construct within Nature, built by man so that the law of the jungle is abandoned and even the weak have rights. Within culture, it is not about the survival of the fittest. Every act is regulated by duties and responsibilities. A structure is created based on standards which distinguish the good from the bad, the right from the wrong, the acceptable from the unacceptable, the appropriate from the inappropriate. Culture works hard to appropriate all that is good and acceptable, all that contributes to stability and order. Culture strives continuously to abandon all that is bad, wrong, unacceptable and inappropriate, all that threatens the sense of permanence and predictability. Over time, culture invalidates all that it rejects. Standards shove all that is undesirable outside the threshold, into the subconscious. Kali stands on the frontier of culture, reminding of all things in Nature that are repressed, suppressed, denied because of fear, standards and judgements.

Kali is a reminder of the fragility of culture. She is

the goddess of war—war represents the collapse of all that culture seeks to uphold. She is the goddess of death—death represents the failure of cultural boundaries to keep out things that pollute and decay. She is the goddess who is naked—nakedness represents the collapse of modesty that culture tries so hard to impose. Kali is the goddess who steps on her husband, challenging patriarchal values that form the foundation of most societies.

For the sage, the idea of the Devi taking blood closes the loop that opens when the Devi gives milk. Thus, the idea of the bloodthirsty Kali complements the image of the milk-giving Gauri, the motherly form of the Devi. Together they make up the cycle of life.

Nothing in Nature appears spontaneously. Everything is a transformation of something else. According to Tantra, the essence of mineral is transformed by plants into sap which is then consumed by animals and humans as food. In the body of animals and humans, sap transforms into plasma, flesh, bone, nerves, semen and blood. Thus all things in Nature are different forms of the same essence.

A popular form of Kali is Dakshina-Kali, which means 'Kali who comes from the south'. According to *Vastu Shastra*, south is the direction of death and change, hence the source of uncertainty, restlessness, insecurity and fear. Facing the south is Shiva in the form of

Dakshina-murti—a teacher who sits under the banyan tree, facing the south. As teacher, Shiva is the source of wisdom; the banyan tree is the ancient symbol of permanence. Shiva's wisdom or gyan calms the mind of the sage so that he can turn south and transform Kali from the source of fear to the cause of bliss.

Conclusion

Conclusion

For most people, the divine is associated with beauty and love. Images of gods and goddesses are therefore expected to please the eye and the heart. Kali, however, defies these expectations. She is neither beautiful nor loving; she is dark, gaunt, and bloodthirsty. Her form takes one by surprise—frightening at first, then confounding. Kali forces a re-examination of all preconceived notions associated with divinity.

Re-examination of the notion of divinity leads to re-considering one's understanding of the world. For, in the Hindu scheme of things, divinity cannot be distinguished from the world: world is divine and divinity is world.

In *Puranas* and *Tantras*, male deities represent the spiritual world while female deities represent the material world. God is the spirit within, Goddess, the substance without; God observes, Goddess is the observation; God sees, Goddess is the scenery. Goddess is the world around, stimulating God into action, flooding God with emotions and ideas, until God realizes himself. Thus world-understanding leads to self-understanding which leads to God-realization.

Devi, the Goddess, embodies nature. Nature is wild and free until culture comes along, disciplines and domesticates her with laws, ethics and values. The forest becomes a field as culture decides what must be in and what must be out. Culture judges, making some things beautiful, some ideas good, and some actions appropriate. The rest become ugly, bad or inappropriate. A time comes when judgements are perceived as natural. Society forgets that its opinions are based on artificial parameters. Society thus prejudices everyone's worldview. Even nature, hence the Devi, comes to be seen through culture's eye.

This eye insists that nature is beautiful and bountiful: the serene wisdom-bestowing Saraswati playing her lute or the enchanting wealth-bestowing Lakshmi with her pot of gold and grain. The world-embodying Devi comes to be visualized as Mangala-Gauri, auspicious and motherly. She is worshipped as Durga, fiercely protective of her children. Then Kali comes along, searing the vision of seers: naked with hair unbound, copulating in the open, killing and drinking blood. She overturns the cart of divine imagery and becomes the grit in culture's eye.

Culture struggles to explain Kali. Desperate attempts are made to rationalize her as the 'killer of demons', and the 'protecting mother'. Images are created that edit out her wild sexuality. Paintings embellish her with jewellery meant for tame wives. The men she decapitates are depicted as outlaws and demons. Society does what it has always done—transforming or denying what it cannot, or does not, or will not, understand.

But Kali gives this cultural manipulation a slip. She

remains a dark and wild enigma challenging the seer, the devotee, and the sorcerer, mocking all preconceived notions. She demands acceptance of all that she represents. Her form and narratives about her throw up questions: Why is she dark and naked? Why is her hair unbound? Why does she copulate openly sitting on top of her lover? Why does she drink blood? Why does she favour sorcerers? The answers force us to confront the dark secrets we shove into our subconscious.

Kali is life who feeds on life. Kali is the unbridled and impersonal sex and violence that makes the cycle of existence go round. Kali stirs the consciousness by copulating with Shiva. She is the raw primal power that existed before there were culture and society, before there were law, ethics and morality. She stands beyond the pall of prejudices, values, and judgements. She encompasses the totality of nature and of life, unfettered by social norms and cultural values.

Kali reminds us that beneath our social indoctrination fester thoughts and desires that do not conform to what is culturally appropriate. The beast within us may be tamed but if we deny its existence or repress it beyond a point, it may slip out and strike, manifesting as rape or riot. Hidden in our hearts are ideas that may not be spoken, but need, at the very least, silent acknowledgement.

Beneath the mask, beneath the self-denial and the self-discipline exists a Kali in all of us.

Hymns

Hymn 1

    Mother of all creation, Kali
    Hear me Maha Kali
    You are the dark cavern
    The source of light
    The forest carpet
    The cause of life
    Heaven's wrath
    The torch and the knife
    Save us from traps
    Grant us truth
    Dance for us, with flute and drum,
    Make the land throb under your feet
    Come down, mother
    Make us complete
    Shatter our bodies, Kali
    Take us home.

               —*New Age Hymn* (Twentieth Century)

Hymn 2

    Awake, Mother!
    Rise
    Long have you been asleep
    Let the *muladhara* bloom
    Rise Mother,
    Let the thousand-petalled lotus bloom in the head

Quick,
Swiftly pierce the six lotuses
And take away my grief, O Essence of
Consciousness!
—*Ramakrishna* (Nineteenth Century)

Hymn 3

Oh Tara, ferry of the soul,
Get me across
Don't know how to swim
My body—a worn-out boat,
Laden with sin.
What can I grasp, what can I do?
How do I cross
This ocean of existence
On my own.
Benares—that's where I should be
Live a pious life
Wait to die.
But here I am
In the river of desire
Far is either shore
Drowning
You are the ferryman in the middle
My only hope.
—*Kalidas Bhattacharya* (Nineteenth Century)

Hymn 4

Mother,
There is ink on my hands,
Ink on my face,
Neighbours laugh.
I see Ma in Shyama
I see Kali in ink
In the multiplication tables I see nothing
But the black kali (ink).
Sound of alphabets
I couldn't care less for
For there isn't among them
Your dark lovely shade
But Mother, I can read
All that you write
On the leaves,
On the waters,
In the ledger that is the sky.
Let them call me illiterate.

—*Kazi Nazrul Islam* (Nineteenth Century)

Hymn 5

I cling to your feet,
You never look at me.
Lost in your own play,
Engrossed in your own emotions,
What is this sport you revel in

Across three worlds?
The universe shuts its eyes in terror,
And calls out 'Mother, Mother!'
Clutching your feet.
In your hands, Kali,
Is the fire of dissolution.
Under your feet
Lies unconscious, the great Shiva.
Wild laughter issues from your mouth
Streams of blood flow down your limbs.
Tara, forgiving one, end our fear!
Pick me up like a baby in your arms.
Come shining like a star,
Smile,
Put a fair dress,
Like dawn after a pitch-black night!
All these days, O Terrible Kali,
I've worshipped only you.
My puja is done, Mother.
Won't you put down your sword?

—*Dvijendralal Ray* (Nineteenth Century)

Hymn 6

You play tricks, Kali.
I know.
You let them call you anything.
Magas call you Pharatara,

Europeans call you God;
Mughals and Pathans,
Saiyids and Qazis
All call you Khuda.
You are Shakti for Shaktas
Shiva for Shaivas
Surya for Sauras
Radha for Vaishnavas
Ganesh for Ganapatyas
Kuber for Yakshas
Vishwakarma for craftsmen
The saint Badar, for boatmen
Ramdulal says this is no delusion.
From what comes to pass,
Truth is felt
But the mind misbehaves
Takes the One to be many.
                    —*Ramdulal Nandi* (Nineteenth Century)

Hymn 7

Hope of hopes—that human rebirth,
But my arrival brought me nothing.
I hover like the bee around a lotus painting,
Hoping for nectar.
You tricked me mother
Gave me bitter neem, saying it is sugar
You cheated me.

You put me on earth saying
'It's time for us to play,'
But the game brought disappointment,
No fun.
Perhaps this was meant to be
Such is the game of existence.
Take me home, mother
Night falls
I am tired.

            —*Ramprasad Sen* (Eighteenth Century)

Hymn 8

O Mother,
You give birth
You protect
You kill
Absorbing all
You are the creator
You are the protector
You are the destroyer
I bow to you, Kali
Beloved of Time
Saviour
Wisdom
Tara
Srividya
Giver of riches

Path of Liberation
Hara and Hari salute you
And all the gods
As do I.
                    —*Karpuradi Stotra* (Seventeenth Century)

Hymn 9

Hrim, destroyer of time!
Srim, embodiment of terror!
Krim, giver of boons!
Mother of Time
Brilliant as the fires of dissolution
Tawny, Black, Night of darkness
Beloved of the creator
Liberator from the bonds of desire
Bearer of the crescent moon
Destroyer of fear, of sin, of pride, in the *Kali* Age
Virginal
Tender
Slender
Lover of wine
Joyous one
Revealer of the path of the Kaulikas
Queen of Kashi
Allayer of sufferings.
To Thee I pay obeisance.
                    —*Adya Kali Stotra* (Sixteenth Century)

Acknowledgements

This book is based on the lectures and writings of my brother Dr Devdutt Pattanaik. I am merely the compiler. May Kali, the dark mother, look upon this endeavour with grace.